Dedication

To my good friend and mentor

the late

Dr. David Koehler

Acknowledgments:

Before you get into the meat of the book, I would like to extend a heartfelt thank you to all who have helped me as I struggled to put this book together! My wife being the first, having put up with my Kokanee Obsession! I would also like to thank my good friend Flora Hovenden for checking my grammar and giving me helpful input as I worked through this book. I have made some strong friendships within the tackle industry and I am deeply in debt to them for their input and support as I slogged through this manuscript. Vance Staplin of Vance's Tackle spent many hours on the phone as well as providing a lot of tackle and tips. Gary Mirales owner of Shasta Tackle provided insight and knowledge as well as a whole lot of tackle. Gary also has been a great inspiration here in the Northwest with his physical and monetary support of the Oregon Kokanee Power organization. Leo and Dana Van Sistine, owners of Sep's Pro Fishing generously sent tackle to use during the course of this book. Bob Schmidt and Bobby Loomis of Mack's Lure met me at Wallowa Lake and generously contributed tackle to the cause. Kyle Neeser of Crystal Basin Tackle not only contributed tackle but spent a whole lot of time on the phone during his busy season helping me out! Dick Murphy of "Fishing With Father Murphy" also contributed some tackle to the cause. Last but not least, Robbie Thorson of R&K Spinners shared many hours out on the lake giving freely of himself and his tackle to see this project through. I would also like to thank Chester Jahn who camped with me up at Wallowa Lake and shared the evening campfire. This guy is one of those fellows who put fish in the boat when nobody else is even getting a bump. His son Jeremy and his grandson also bring a smile to my face as I look back over the year leading up to this book. Mike Mansker a fellow member of kokaholics anonymous did his best to keep me on the straight and narrow, a task which I might add is a substantial one (just ask my wife)! I know that I have missed some of the people who have helped and I apologize for that!

Introduction

Over the years my passion for chasing Kokanee has surpassed the boiling point almost every season. The more I chase this fish, the less I seem to know about them. I have read everything I can lay my hands on, attended every seminar that has come to the area, attended countless Sportsman's shows, talked to the tackle makers, bugged my fellow fishermen on the dock, the ramp and out on the water trying to master this elusive prey and still feel the need to know more! I spend every opportunity on the water (three to four days a week on average) trying this lure and that spinner, messing with dodger and flasher combinations, water temperature and what have you. Through all of this, one thing is obvious, the more I learn about this great game fish the more I am hooked.

I started fishing for Kokanee as a kid growing up in central Oregon. They were great fun at that time and since my folks only were able to get us to the coast for a couple of weeks every summer, they ended up being my main focus as I grew older and before I relocated to the Willamette Valley. My how things have changed since that time! Tackle, equipment and knowledge have come a long way since that time which led up to writing this book.

If you do participate in this wonderful fishery on a full time basis, I would highly encourage you to get involved with the Kokanee Power organization. These are the folks who will help keep our fishery on track as well as exposing kids to something other than video games and TV.

I do not claim to be the best fisherman; I am merely a fellow fisherman who is interested in furthering the sport.

During final revisions, I realized that I did not have photos of myself fishing. I trust that will not be a problem for the reader.

I hope you can glean some helpful tips from the following pages and that your significant other will either participate with you or understand your need to fill multiple tackle boxes with gear. If you do gain some knowledge from these pages, possibly you can return the favor by getting someone else infected with this Kokanee Obsession thing!

~Tight Lines and Good Fishing~
  Kent Cannon

All inquiries should be addressed to:
Kent Cannon Enterprises.LLC
4742 Liberty Rd. S. #344
Salem, OR 97302-5000
All photos taken by the author unless otherwise noted.
SB ISBN-10 13: 0-615-43390-1   SB ISBN- 9780615433905

1 ...An Introduction to Kokaholics

Years ago, I was fishing on Wickiup Reservoir located in the Deschutes National forest of central Oregon. I had been out on the lake since just before sunup and I was planning on heading for home later in the day. I was getting in a few last moments of fishing before returning to the grind of the working world. While fishing that morning I had what I thought was decent success, having boated several real nice Kokanee in the neighborhood of 16-18 inches all of which were on ice in a cooler in the front of the boat.

Shortly after 10:00 AM another boat began fishing alongside me and proceeded to catch fish like I had never witnessed before. Pass after pass I watched this other angler land one large Kokanee after another. I tried everything I had in the box trying to duplicate his success. But try as I might, my results were dismal in comparison. Instead of getting frustrated, I started paying attention; I stopped the boat, pulled out the binoculars and started taking lessons as I watched this guy clean up on the Kokanee.

The difference between this day and countless others in which I had tried everything in the tackle box trying to match what the more successful fishermen were using was that I started looking at the big picture. The light had come on and hopefully it would never go out again! Countless times I had the same scene play out in front of my eyes and only paid attention to small parts of the whole. I had read everything I could get my hands on, bought a huge tackle box worth of gear which was guaranteed to catch fish, put in countless hours on lake and stream but up until that moment, I had not been able to stand back and see everything that was going on.

How many times have you been out on the lake and seen someone just raking in the fish at a rate which would surely sink their boat if they continued? Have you asked them what they were using? Did you stop and listen patiently while they explained how they were using it and why?

Shortly after that <u>LIGHTBULB MOMENT</u> ☼, I started keeping a journal of my fishing adventures. I write down my daily catch in a log; time of day, weather conditions, barometer, depth, water temperature, lure, bait, and scent used etc… I use that information every time I go fishing. I can look up a year ago under the same or similar conditions and see a pattern. The longer I do this the more I am able to tie this information into the life pattern of the Kokanee or any other fish which I target during the course of the year. Your journal doesn't need to be fancy; it can be as simple as a spiral notebook or a stenographer's pad. If you are one of those high tech guys, you can keep the information on a PDA. It doesn't matter what format you use, just include the pertinent information in a format which you can understand. Get in the habit of doing it every time you go fishing. I do mine, sitting in the truck after the day has ended; the boat is on the trailer and the gear put away. Another good time to do it is while waiting in line to pull your boat out of the water. I can't emphasize this enough; **just do-it**, the payoff will come sooner than you think! What gets written down gets remembered!

Just after the first of the year, while fishing a local lake. I was having good success and enjoying the day, just myself and my fishing buddy, Rocky, who happens to be my dog. There was another boat out on the lake fishing with the usual pop gear, and probably a wedding ring with worms or corn. It looked to me like a grandfather & grandson spending the day together. Shortly after noon, they cruised by and in passing asked if I was having any luck. I told them yes, I was doing fairly well and would be heading in soon. The older fellow told me they hadn't seen a fish all day and asked what I was using. About that time I got another take down and they waited patiently while I landed my latest fish. Once I was able to talk freely, I told them what I was using and started to tell them how I was using it. The only thing they heard was Apex, not how it was being used or why; throwing their boat in gear and motoring off to have more of the same luck or in this case no luck at all.

Men are terrible at taking directions, just ask my wife. She will figure out where we need to go, how to get there, the best route and the time it will take.

I get in the car, and head in the general direction of the place I am going, I don't get lost or at least that is what I tell my wife. I don't have a clue about how to get there and I don't ask for directions until I am hopelessly lost and then I can't understand why she gets upset. It must be one of those men are from Mars and women are from Venus things! The same is true when I take someone fishing. The women listen; want to know all of the details, why this happens and why that works when this doesn't. Men get in the boat and usually don't pay any attention to what you tell them even if they ask you specific questions. They almost always go back to doing it the way they have always done it when things don't work out just the way they think it should have. In short, they only want to know the destination not how to get there. The good news is this thought process can be changed, I am living proof!

Men going fishing live out the same scenario on the water as the one outlined above, we buy the cool tackle, nice boat, neat clothing, and high-tech waders then all of a sudden we are fishermen. Forget about not knowing how to fish, we will figure it out on the way. It may take years or just never happen, that is, unless we stop and ask the right questions to find our way and then many times we will only listen to what we think is important and not what, where, when and why.

One of my Kokanee fishing friends, Mike Mansker, calls it, "becoming a student of the fish." My LIGHTBULB MOMENT ☼ My Wickiup experience years ago made even more sense after he put it in context. The more I fish, the more I pay attention to the bite and what causes it. Mike related how a goldfish would suck in a fish pellet and spit it out several times before it would actually eat the pellet and move on to another. Have you ever watched the rod tip bob up and down slightly as a fish sampled your offering before grabbing the pole giving ripping hook-set on the rod, only to miss the fish? If so, this should be a LIGHTBULB MOMENT ☼ for you! Over the course of the next several chapters I will be giving you some tips on how to do this and how to do that, but if you don't listen to the whole story it will be just like the hook-set just mentioned, you will miss the fish or in this case, the lesson!

Stocking:

Kokanee, a land locked version of the sockeye salmon, found from Alaska all the way down through Northern California were introduced by stocking in some Western lakes as early as the 1920's. Naturally occurring Kokanee are found predominantly in Alaska, Canada, Japan and Siberia.

Thanks to stocking, the fish are now found in over 200 lakes dispersed over California, Idaho,

Oregon, New Mexico, Wyoming, Utah and Montana. Kokanee are what I like to think of as a terminal fishery. For me that means if I land the fish it is going home in the cooler. The reasoning for this is twofold:

a.) Kokanee do not fare well in a catch and release situation compared to trout. They have a tendency to go belly up when released even when it is carefully done, and for that reason some states have adopted the fish landed rule with no minimum size.

b.) Unlike the varieties of trout found in the same lakes, Kokanee are destined to die in three to four years on average. They are prolific breeders and will overpopulate a lake in short order if allowed to do so. By keeping your catch you are insuring the remaining fish in the lake will attain full size by their spawning year.

In lakes where the fish are allowed to over populate, they are usually small, sometimes as small as six inches at maturity. By applying fishing pressure to these fish you enable them to gain in size, sometimes into the twenty inch range.

Many lakes contain self-sustaining populations of Kokanee. Lakes with the proper habitat for spawning can have very robust Kokanee fisheries. There are also lakes which require stocking every year much like the rainbow fisheries in many of the States. The reasoning for planting Kokanee in specific lakes vary although one very good reason is that they eat the plankton and in the process can and will out feed certain trash fish introduced to those lakes either accidentally or on purpose by other fishermen.

Biology:

While primarily plankton eaters, Kokanee will occasionally eat other things, such as bugs, fly larvae and small crustaceans although it is done for the most part only in the spring. Kokanee feed on plankton by straining the small zooplankton from the water with their gill rakers. Trout, chinook and silver salmon and other predatory fish all have short, widely spaced gill rakers. When in question as to whether it is a Kokanee or Chinook for example, it is easy to lift the gill plate on a fish and view the gill rakers. This is one of the easiest and most fool proof methods of determining the difference between Kokanee and other similar looking fish. (See Illustration 1)

Spawning habitat for Kokanee can either be in a lake or river. For example, in 1981 and 1982 the planting of a stream spawning strain of kokanee in Don Pedro Lake in La Grange,

Illustration 1: This is a photo of a Kokanee gill. Note the bottom of the gill (bottom of photo) has long spines sticking out. The Kokanee use these to strain the plankton from the water. By lifting the gill plate you can easily see whether the fish is a Kokanee or not. Trout, Chinook and Silver salmon have short gill rakers.

California. These kokanee never returned to the natal stream. It was assumed the population did not survive until two fish were caught by legendary kokanee fisherman Phil Johnson. It was later determined the fish were spawning in the gravel beds of the lake.

Kokanee are known to exist side by side with their close cousins the Sockeye, in some of the northern lakes. Because of this, it strikes a hole in the theory that kokanee became land locked by geological occurrences. Studies have also shown that not all wild spawning sockeye return to the ocean. Some of those fish will linger on in the nursery lake for their entire existence, schooling up with their ocean-run brothers and sisters at the appropriate time in the fall to spawn.

The kokanee fishery has proven to be a very important part of many western lakes, providing a food source for larger, more aggressive fish such as the lake trout and land locked Chinook salmon while also consuming the algae or plankton in competition with less favorable *trash* fish. The spawning fish in the fall replenish the streams, rivers and lakes with nutrients and required minerals with their spawned out carcasses. They also provide an important food source for eagles, foxes, mink, fisher, and minnows; not to mention many other forest animals, birds and insects needed to maintain a healthy ecological balance.

Although Kokanee have been planted in many lakes from Alaska all of the way down to California, not all of the populations still exist even though they were prolific and had stable populations in the beginning. One of the main reasons for this was the introduction of the Mysis shrimp more commonly called the Opossum shrimp. In 1949 the shrimp were introduced experimentally into Kootenay Lake in British Columbia, Canada to enhance the trout population. What the survey showed was a dramatic increase in the growth rate and size of the Kokanee salmon. Subsequently the shrimp were introduced into over 100 other lakes in the Western United States and Canada primarily to stimulate Kokanee growth. The Opossum shrimp are voracious predators of the same zooplankton which Kokanee rely on for a food source. The shrimp, originally intended as a food source for the Kokanee maintains a distinctly different lifestyle which allows the shrimp to radically increase in abundance and in the process out-compete the Kokanee for their primary food source. The Kokanee for the most part feed in the early morning and early evening. Kokanee remain fairly constant in the water column during the peak of the zooplankton production, stratified at the thermo cline (This topic will be covered in depth later in the chapter). The Opossum shrimp on the other hand feed at night while Kokanee are fairly dormant and then move down to the bottom during the day thus avoiding predation by the Kokanee. In Kootenay Lake, at the time of their introduction upwelling currents brought the shrimp into some of the shallower waters of the lake making them available for the Kokanee to feed on during their prime feeding hours. That situation has now changed due to the building of a large upstream dam, the reduction of the nutrient load of the lake and the loss of the upwelling currents. Some lakes affected by the Mysis shrimp have stabilized and started down the road to recovery while others have never recovered and still lack a viable Kokanee population. One of the Northwest lakes where conditions have been optimal for the shrimp and the Kokanee populations to coexist is Wallowa Lake in Eastern Oregon near Joseph. At the writing of this book, the Oregon state record has been broken four times and the US record has been broken twice. That happened over the course of only seven months. The size of the fish being taken on the lake is in direct correlation to the fish feeding on Opossum shrimp and the obvious balance between the two. Flathead Lake in Montana is a good example of a fishery gone awry by the introduction of the shrimp; going from a highly productive lake, consistently yielding over 100,000 fish to anglers prior to the introduction of the Opossum shrimp to barely 6000 fish within three short years of the shrimps' introduction.

Another cause of downfall in many lakes is the predation by lake trout or Mackinaw. Predations by lake trout in combination with competition from the Mysis shrimp for food are the key causes of the demise of Kokanee populations in several lakes across the West. With increased catch limits and bounties for lake trout in conjunction with stocking programs, the state of Idaho has shown that Kokanee populations can recover. Lake Pend Oreille in Idaho is a prime example of a recovering Kokanee habitat. Predation by Mackinaw and Rainbow trout were not the only factor in the crash of this lake. Winter draw down of water levels exposed spawning beds, forcing juvenile fish out into the lake where they were more susceptible to predators. By better controlling the water levels in conjunction with reducing predator levels the lake is now seeing a surprising comeback. So you see it is not a simple problem when you look into what is causing the crash of a Kokanee population and knee jerk reactions can even make the situation worse. It is only by careful observation leading to carefully administered adjustments to stabilize a foundering population.

Life pattern:

The life pattern of the Kokanee is very important if you want to become successful student of the fish and consistently catch more fish! Kokanee live a fairly consistent life based on the cycles of the seasons coupled with the simple fact that they are destined to die within three to four years on average, depending on their environment and the strain of Kokanee. This consistent lifestyle gives the Kokanee angler a distinct advantage when targeting this fish. Depending on what season you are fishing, you will know where and how to catch fish regardless of the lake you are fishing anywhere in North America and elsewhere in the world where Kokanee are found.

Water Properties affecting Kokanee:

Water differs from most other compounds because it is less dense as a solid than as a liquid. Consequently ice floats, while water at temperatures just above freezing sinks. Water is most dense at 39.2°F and becomes less dense at both higher and lower temperatures. Because of this density-temperature relationship, many lakes in temperate climates tend to stratify, forming into distinct layers. This stratification is very important to the Kokanee fisherman.

Spring Season:

Spring Turnover is when the picture really changes. In the spring when the lake turns over and the ice goes away the fish move into the shallower portions of the lake in search of food, ending their state of semi-dormancy. During this period, Kokanee feed with voracity on a variety of larvae and bugs. It is during this period that Kokanee can be taken much by accident by those targeting trout and other species. It is also one of the easiest periods to catch Kokanee. During this period, you can catch them by Jigging, bait fishing, and trolling.

The fish will inhabit sheltered bays, shallow grassy areas, the points off inlets and in the case of larger lakes with predominant strong winds, the shallow areas which the wind pushes the warmer surface waters into.

A fellow Kokanee addict told me of a time when he and his wife were fishing the downwind end of Suttle lake in Central Oregon one spring day. There were thirty boats, each with at least two fishermen. Everyone caught their limits inside of an hour. He told me that you could have thrown a hubcap over the side and caught fish. This is a prime example of spring fishing on a lake with a strong predominant wind. During this spring period, the fish are bunched up into schools and dining on a smorgasbord of invertebrates such as fresh water shrimp, mayflies, damsel flies and Chironomids (which are the larvae of the common midge). Invertebrates are basically tied to the bottom while the Chironomids rise in a tiny gas bubble and are picked off by the fish as they float to the surface. The next phase of spring lake development is the phytoplankton. Phytoplankton are algae which swim or float in water. They include single-cells, colonies of cells, and filaments (linear strings of cells) which are usually capable of photosynthesis. Many protozoa are closely related to algae, so the distinction between protozoa and algae is artificial.

As soon as the phytoplankton is in full swing the zooplankton start to multiply while feeding off the phytoplankton. Zooplankton is dominated by four major groups of animals: protozoa, rotifers, and two subclasses of Crustacea; the cladocerans and copepods. Once the zooplankton is in abundant supply the Kokanee will spread out over the lake feeding like cattle out on a green field.

When the Kokanee start feeding off the zooplankton, and spread out over the lake they are into what I call the summer phase of the year. This will be the longest phase and arguably the hardest time to target Kokanee because they are dispersed over the lake. The reason I say hardest is because the fish now become accessible to more targeted means due to the depth the fish will be found at.

LIGHTBULB MOMENT ☼: A good habit to get into, especially in the spring is to open up the stomach of the Kokanee and look to see what it is they are eating. Once they get into zooplankton they start to disperse, signaling the change of seasons. By being aware of what the Kokanee are eating, you will be aware of where they are in relation to the season.

Summer Season:

Once the summer season starts, the fish will spread out over the lake feeding on their food of choice, zooplankton. The key here is, the warmer the water gets the deeper the fish will go. Kokanee prefer water in the 50° to 55° range. They will be found sometimes in warmer water and sometimes in cooler water but for the most part they will stay right in this comfort range if they are allowed by lake conditions such as depth. As the surface temperature continues to rise, you will see, if you have good electronics, a distinct layer called a thermo cline. The thermo cline as defined by Merriam-Webster is: *the region in a thermally stratified body of water which separates warmer surface water from cold deep water and in which temperature decreases rapidly with depth.* Note: Review the paragraph just before *Spring Season*. In my experience the fish will sit right at or just below this line. They will come up to warmer water to feed and then go back and hang right below this layer or line in the water.

One key to this thermo cline is that this is where there is oxygen rich water and an ideal breeding ground for zooplankton production. By locating this layer you can effectively target Kokanee even when you cannot see them on your fish finder.

LIGHTBULB MOMENT ☼: You can also find this ideal temperature with a simple thermometer which you can purchase for little or nothing at your sporting goods supply. The thermometer has a glass tube with a valve which will also give you a depth reading. Remember back when discussing keeping a log, I commented on water temperature? By using this simple device you can get accurate

Find Feeding fish faster with...

DEPTHERM
Depth & Temperature

information.

For you movie buffs, In the Hunt for Red October the subs were hiding below this layer because the sonar will bounce off the layer where the cold water meets the warm water if the sonar beam is at a shallow angle. You can find this layer with a good fish finder/sonar by turning up the sensitivity. It will show up on your graph as a line with interference not to be confused with the lines left by your downrigger weights. This will be covered in detail in Chapter 2 under GPS/Sonar.

Even though the fish are spread out over the lake, they will still be found in specific areas more times than not. Once I fish a lake, and learn the spots that consistently produce fish for me I keep track of those locations in my journal as well as marking them with my GPS. If one area is not producing I will move to another.

There is no point in presenting your offerings to the open water with no fish around to appreciate the fine lures and bait on the end of your line. Kokanee are funny fish in that they will be thick in one area for several days and then one day they will up and move for no apparent reason. I used to just start trolling as soon as I could get into deep water. That meant it could be ten minutes until I found fish or it could be two hours. My routine now is to motor to known producing areas (usually away from everyone else) and idle through while watching the fish finder. Once I have determined what area holds good numbers of fish I will then go ahead and fish it. If I am not marking good quantities of fish, I move on to my next hot spot and repeat the process. I

Robbie Thorson with a nice catch of Kokanee at Green Peter Reservoir

don't waste time fishing an area just because I did well in that location last time I was at the lake. This train of thought is similar to the guy that landed a huge fish on a specific lure. Time after time he uses the same lure as his go-to presentation. He catches fish occasionally on that lure but the days when he goes home without fish he thinks the bite is off, when in reality he is stuck in a rut and not taking into consideration that maybe the fish weren't biting that color that specific day. My point in all of this is to encourage you to think outside the box. Cut down on the time you are fishing unproductive water and spend your time fishing water where the fish are eager to get into your boat!

Fall:

Late summer will again find the fish schooling up. However, the areas in which you will find them will not be the same as in the spring. You will now find them staging to spawn even though the spawn is still quite a ways off. By this time the fish which are to spawn this year will have pretty much reached full size. The jaw will show distinct hooking in the males and the females will show similar traits although not as pronounced. Planted fish in lakes which have no areas suitable area for spawning will still assemble into tight schools and exhibit spawning behavior including the physical changes. Locate these schools and you will have located your next meal!

As the season progresses the spawning male's heads will turn green and the sides and back will turn pink or even red with a dirty white belly. The female will also turn color although again not as pronounced and will be pink to copper on the sides with more green on the back.

As the fish get closer to spawning they become much more aggressive. By this time they will strike a lure out of anger more than anything else. Once somewhat timid they are now more ready to attack, possibly because they are getting into the; "protect the nest mode" or chase off the other male while vying for the female that has your eye "mode."

During this phase of their lives Kokanee are still susceptible to fishermen. The presentation is slightly different since the fish have for the most part quit feeding. The males will be the most aggressive. Larger flashier lures and dodgers are the rule of thumb. They are now conserving their strength for the run up the natal stream to spawn so presentations will need to be slower, requiring less energy to pursue and more tuned towards inciting aggressive behavior.

The fish which are to spawn will start to absorb organs not needed during the rest of their lifespan. They will eventually either absorb or lose their scales and become covered with slime or mucus.

You will find these fish lying off the mouths of spawning creeks where the cool water from the streams enters the lake. They will lay in the bottom of underwater valleys where cooler water is found while waiting for the fall rains that will give them the opportunity to enter the creeks and rivers of their natal streams. Once the fish enter the streams, they are for the most part not worth pursuing. They are essentially the living dead and not worthy of table fare. Note also fish with the distinct color changes indicated above are probably not worth targeting. Slight pink is fine but beyond that, the fish are better left to spawn. Those who intentionally target spawning fish (pink with humpy backs and green heads) cause great damage to the fishery!

Winter Season:

During the winter, Kokanee typically suspend in the lower water column and become somewhat dormant wasting as little energy as possible. There is less food source available at that time since zooplankton the primary food source of the Kokanee is reduced

As the weather cools during late fall, the upper water is wind mixed and cooled, reducing the density difference between it and the layer below the thermo cline, which is the most stable layer due to water density (Refer back to *Water Properties*). As time passes, winds turn over and mix the lake to greater depths, and the thermo cline or layer where the temperature difference is the most pronounced during the summer time, gradually deepens. When surface and bottom waters approach the same temperature and density, fall winds can mix the entire lake; leading to the condition known as "fall turn over." As the atmosphere cools, the surface water continues to cool until it freezes. At this point a less distinct density stratification than seen in summer develops under the ice. Most of the water column is fairly constant at a temperature of 39.20°F, which is denser than the colder, lighter water just below the ice. In this case where water is broken into distinct layers due to water density the layering is much less stable, because the density difference between 32°F and 39.2°F water is quite small. The water column is isolated from wind-induced upwelling and mixing by the cap of ice, therefore, this layering persists throughout the winter.

Contrary to the popular belief there is little to no zooplankton production during the winter season, studies have shown that although reduced, zooplankton is still available and the fish do feed during the winter. Due to cooler temperatures the digestion process in winter Kokanee is much slower than in the spring through the fall of the year. A study, conducted by Steinhart and Wurtsbaugh over two winters showed that Kokanee were actively feeding throughout the winter months although length and weight changes varied between the two years studied. This was indicative of prey abundance (zooplankton) between the two winters. The less prey, the less active the fish became in order to conserve their energy resources. The inactivity or lessened activity took place in late November and seemed to increase the following months leading towards the following spring. The more zooplankton abundance the less active the fish became possibly due to the fact that it was not necessary to graze as much (due to the slower winter metabolism).

Kokanee can be targeted through the ice or by boat during this period. While fishing in this fashion, jigging or still bait fishing will be your most productive method of catching fish although trolling can still be fun and produce fish.

What Stimulates Kokanee to Bite?

There are many theories and personal beliefs out there as to why a fish which is a known non-predator would attack a lure or spinner with such a vengeance. The truth is there are few if any who really know. However we can analyze patterns of behavior and come up with a pretty accurate theory. Based on the season, targeted depth is the key factor in continually and successfully catching Kokanee. Kokanee are a cold water specie much like their fellow ocean-run cousins and as such have specific needs in regards to temperature.

The truth is you will find most Kokanee in water no warmer than 55 degrees. They will enter warmer water while feeding but due to their temperature requirements for survival, they cannot spend extended periods in warmer water without terminal effects. By the same token, Kokanee will not typically be found in water temperatures below the mid forty ranges (Fahrenheit) during the lion's share of the year. Keeping temperature in mind, you can locate

Kokanee at any given time of the year by watching water temperature. Note: remember the

thermometer mentioned in the Summer Section? The next stimulant is season which will give you some idea as to how to effectively target them based on their feeding patterns during each of the four seasons covered earlier in this chapter. For example, in the spring the fish are usually located in shallow water, in schools, and feeding voraciously on bugs and larvae. You can target these three things, location, voracity of feeding and the fact that they are schooled up to narrow down the presentation.

Something which really makes me wonder is: why someone who trolls refuses to jig and vise versa! Another interesting conundrum is why neither a jigger nor a troller will try still bait fishing even though it may be the most effective way to target the fish in a certain period. Quite honestly, this ain't politics so you can cross party lines, at least in the case of Kokanee fishing!

Sound/Vibration:

There are four stimulants which stimulate a bite: vibration/sound, sight, color and scent. The most important of those is (again in my opinion) sound. In this case sound translates to vibration which is I believe how a fish senses sound. Kokanee, being a non-predator, are constantly aware of their surroundings mostly in an effort to avoid becoming dinner for a predator and to maintain personal space. Keeping in mind, vibrations/sounds that imitate a dying bait fish are probably not positive sounds to a Kokanee. On the other hand, sounds which imitate a smaller fish moving through a Kokanee's personal space are likely to invite a strike. One of the reasons for this, after watching fish interact for hours and hours in a fish tank, is that some of the most aggressive fish on the earth are plankton feeders. They are known as fin nippers to those that raise exotic fish. Cichlids, a species of fish found all over the world in various sub species have proven to be extremely aggressive, and exceedingly so, a fish found in Malawi Lake in Africa. Cichlids are aggressive to the point of attacking another fish intruding on its space and killing the intruder. When your lure penetrates a Kokanee's space they perceive as their own causes them to go into attack mode to run off the intruder. Hence the sudden strike. By the same token, a vibration/sound which indicates a larger fish brings on a defensive posture which in the case of Kokanee is to flee.

LIGHTBULB MOMENT ☼: Try running a full size salmon dodger on one side of your boat in a lake known for predatory fish, either lake trout or Bull trout. That side will show little if any fish the entire time the larger dodger is in place! Both of these two behaviors were caused by vibration/sound. Both of these two examples will play a key role in putting fish in the boat, each in its own way.

When your presentation is not getting bit, look at size. Sometimes in areas of high predation (as in lakes where there are lake trout or bull trout), the fish are skittish from being attacked. Small presentations with smaller vibration patterns will be more likely to encourage a bite. Sometimes the reverse of that is true. In lakes with little predation the fish are not bothered as much by larger presentations and more flash.

Sight is the next most important factor in catching more fish. Once you have the fish's attention with vibration, they are maneuvering to see what it is that is approaching. It is at this point the fish determines the fight or flight mode. Having a color which invites a strike at this moment is the key to your presentation. Kokanee are fickle in their selection of favorite colors. They can change color preference by the minute or the same color can last all day. There is neither rhyme nor reason as to why, at least not by our logic. The primary colors and their variations play a very important role in presentations. The color spectrum, as affected by the water column, will play a key role in selecting a color that is most effective.

Color:

Detroit Lake looking roughly North from the mouth of Divide Creek

Water absorbs light with depth. Clear water will ultimately cancel light at a given depth depending on several factors, even more so, light penetrating through water with plankton bloom. Add to the plankton bloom a slightly choppy surface and you have reduced the amount of light penetration even more. The sunlit layer will actually extend to about 330 feet while most presentations for Kokanee are not over 110 feet. As you descend in the water column, light frequencies are absorbed in the following order, starting with red then orange, then yellow, then green, then blue, then indigo, and the last frequency to disappear is violet. Bearing this in mind, choice of lure color is very important when fishing at depth. Please note; fluorescent and glow colors are not impacted by this degradation of light. Fluorescent and glow colors retain their actual color at depth. On hot summer days with little surface disturbance, I have had extremely good results fishing with Indigo and purple lures at 65 feet. Coincidence? I don't think so, based on the results in my fishing log over the course of several years.

Another interesting factor to consider is UV rays. UV rays will penetrate up to approximately 75 feet (ideal conditions) depending on sun location, surface conditions and clarity of the water. Obviously the clarity will be depreciated by the presence of a large phytoplankton bloom. Another factor to consider here is that UV rays are not degraded by cloud cover so on overcast days UV treated spoons, baits, scents and dyes can be extremely effective.

Scent:

The next component in consistently catching Kokanee is scent. Sockeye salmon travel incredible distances to get to their natal lakes. The reason that they (a fish with a pea sized brain) are able to find their way home to the spawning areas where they originally came from, is scent.

A prime example of the complexity of this sense of smell is the sockeye returning to Redfish Lake in Idaho which is a distance of over 950 miles from the mouth of the Columbia River. The journey is even more complex in that it covers a number of different river systems, each with their own scents. The fish needs to sort out all of the correct scents to end up back where the journey began four years before.

Suttle Lake

One year while fishing with Dan Ponciano on the Columbia the conversation turned to the salmon's sense of smell. Dan made the statement "a salmon's sense of smell is 150 times more powerful than that of a bloodhound," which is renowned for its famous nose. I have never been able to substantiate that but it is still an excellent example of why scent is so important. The first place scent is important, is on your hands and anything which comes in contact with your lure presentation up to and including your fishing line and the hands which touch all of them. Human scent can be a definite repellent when it comes to fishing. Have you ever watched two people fishing in the same boat the same bait and lure and one of the two people catches substantially more fish? Chances are it was not luck; it is very likely the person not catching fish had a scent issue. That is why a serious Kokanee fisherman will not allow anyone to touch his tackle. Scent transfers can and will kill the bite! The constant washing of hands is mandatory in my boat simply because of that.

The makers of Joy dishwashing soap have probably not made a fortune at my expense but I am sure they have made a fair amount! There are many other scents which are associated with killing the bite, one of which is sun screen. Use it on your arms, face and head but never on your hands!

The other end of the scent spectrum are those which are intentionally applied to bait and terminal gear to attract fish. There are many scent products on the market today as opposed to when I started fishing for Kokanee. Most of the scents we used were put together through trial and error and were closely guarded secrets. Those scents are still around today in that some of the older guys have passed them down to the kids who now use those time-honored secrets to this day. Since many who start out in this fanatical Kokanee chasing business do not have access to those secrets, there is a shortcut. Commercially produced scents available over the counter in most good sporting goods stores fill the bill quite nicely. If you have attracted fish through vibrations and sight, why not seal the deal with a little scent? This topic is covered in much more detail in chapter 3.

2 ...The Boat & the Gear

What is it you really need to target Kokanee? What type of boat will work the best and how do you equip it? You might answer these questions with more questions such as how many people are going to be fishing with you and how serious are you about this new hobby? There are many answers to these questions and I am sure, if you are like me, you will find a way to justify the expenses incurred while pursuing this wonderful game fish. The truth is there is no one correct answer; everyone's needs are different. Focusing on the needs of the majority, in the course of this chapter I will lay out a wide variety of choices and it will be up to the reader to pick the ones which not only meet their individual needs but their budget as well. When I started fishing, a fancy boat was one which floated and didn't have to be constantly bailed. Usually it was a wood or aluminum model in the twelve to fourteen foot range with a small, blue smoke belching Evinrude or Johnson or possibly a Mercury outboard motor on the back. The anchor consisted of a coffee can filled with concrete with a short length of chain embedded in the center with a hundred feet of rope attached to that. The seats were wood, usually with no padding other than maybe a jacket or when it was colder a blanket or if you were lucky a floating seat cushion. We didn't have a fish finder and in reality, we didn't even know there was such a thing. You didn't talk because that would allegedly spook the fish and one of the hot baits was Velveeta cheese and a chunk worm or a combo of each of those along with a Pautzke's Ball of Fire. We had never heard of downriggers at that time and the bilge pump was a bucket and you sure as heck hoped you didn't need it! The auto pilot was usually my dad, or a family friend. The toilet facility consisted of a coffee can and a poncho for privacy. There was no such thing as a GPS, temperature gauge or any of those other newfangled inventions. When you were out in the boat you stayed in your seat, not risking walking around and possibly tipping the boat over.

Thank god most of that has changed over the years. Technology has now enabled us to fish in relative comfort and seemingly find the fish with little effort compared to "back in the day." With all of the options today's boat buyer has, the question becomes: what is really important?

Boats:

Cost, comfort, serviceability, motor, and launch ability are all things to seriously consider when buying a boat. How much boat is really needed? If you were to drive around town today in any given neighborhood, you will see many boats which look /like they never get put in the water. They are nice boats, some  are top of the line bought by someone who either thought it would be nice to have a boat or bought on a whim or maybe the rest of the family didn't really enjoy fishing, or any of a number of other excuses. The point remains that the boat is still sitting there gradually losing its value, a reminder of a bad decision made. Buying a boat is a serious decision! Take your time and consider the purchase carefully! Consider where the boat is going to be used and how it is going to be used. Are you going to fish the rivers as well as the salt in addition to lake fishing? Do you want to be able to walk around while fishing or are you comfortable sitting?

Do you need a top to keep out the weather and/or give you shade in the heat of summer? My advice to the first time boat buyer would be to sit down and make a list of the things you would like in a boat. Then make a second list of the things you find absolutely necessary in a boat. Do some shopping online or at a sportsman's show. **_Look but don't buy_**! Take some time and really see what is out there then take your list and modify it into realistic terms in dollars and cents. Definitely consider a used boat. There are lots of boats out there just sitting which can be picked up for a fraction of what that same boat would cost off the showroom floor. The bonus of buying a pre-owned boat is that a lot of the time you can get extras like fish finder, GPS, downriggers, anchors and auto pilot which are the things

Lake Billy Chinook down towards the dam

you will end up buying in addition to the cost of buying a new boat.

I am a welded aluminum boat fan. I like to know that if I bump a rock or floating log the chances are I am not going to be going for a swim. That is not to say that there are not some real cool fiberglass boats out there. I have drooled over several nice glass boats, but it always comes back to the fact that I don't want to have to swim because I wasn't careful. That is a statement about me, and I am trying to be honest. Welded aluminum boats are more expensive than their glass or plastic counterparts so if that is an issue and you are not reckless like me then by all means go with the less expensive alternative.

The next thing to consider is size. The size can be dictated by your budget so if that is the case, buy the boat you can afford which will still accomplish what it is you need it to do. If you live on a large lake, size works one way where if your local lake is a smaller body of water, size works the other. Larger boats are harder to launch and require a more improved ramp whereas a smaller boat can be launched on an unimproved ramp with little effort. Large lakes tend to have some pretty strong winds on occasion which, if you are fishing from a small boat, can be dangerous or at least keep you from fishing until the winds die down. If you are in an area known for high winds, maybe a small boat is not a good decision, kind of like launching a large boat on a puddle of a lake. When looking at size, consider how many people are going to be in the boat and trying to fish. Too small of a boat and you end up tripping over each other. Match the boat size to what you want/need to accomplish!

Another consideration is; do you want an open boat or do you want the windshield? I personally like the windshield because I can troll into the wind without even feeling the breeze. But the elimination of the wind shield means more seating.

One final consideration would be hull shape. This one item is very important especially for those who are considering multiple uses.

A deep V bottom will track straighter and handle better in the wind. However if you are going with multiple use, there are hybrids out there which will provide both the characteristics of the sled (or flat bottom) and the deep V hull. By putting a flat spot on the rear of the hull, you get the advantages of both.

My grandson Matt on a spring trip

Motors:

Boat motors today come in a large assortment of sizes and makes.

Depending on the size of your boat, you may be able to get by with one motor. If you choose to go that route, will the motor be able to idle down to a reasonable trolling speed between .5 and 1.8 Mph and still be able to get up on plane when you need to get from point A to point B? If the wind comes up suddenly is the motor fast enough to move your boat to safety quickly?

My present boat is too large to get by with only one motor. I have the main motor to get me from the dock to the fishing area and a trolling or kicker motor to use when I get there. Having fished my present boat for several years now, there are things that I like about it and things that I wouldn't do again. One of the ones which I wouldn't do again is buy a bigger trolling motor. My boat is only twenty feet long and after fishing out of a guided twenty four boat with five other fishermen and a guide, powered by an eight horse motor which handled the load just fine, I have to say I was misguided when I bought mine. I should have purchased a larger main motor and a smaller kicker or trolling motor or spent the money on accessories.

Another consideration when buying motors for your boat would be whether to go with gas or mixed gas motors. In today's environmentally conscious world, mixed gas or two-stroke engines may be a thing of the past. Alaska opted to ban them altogether from their lakes and rivers and other states may be considering this as well. With that in mind, I would be cautious about spending that kind of money and end up stuck with a motor which is little better than an anchor. It may never happen, but it would be a shame to own one and not be able to use it! Both of the motors on my boat are four strokes. After owning and using two-strokes, I would personally never go back. Four Strokes are quiet, easy starting, don't smoke and run very smooth. From the research I have done, many of the top producers of outboard motors have done some modifications to their line of two-strokes to the point they meet or exceed the EPA rules. Even so, I would be cautious when purchasing one.

I have a jet or pump on my main motor for fishing in the river. Quite honestly with the poor runs of salmon we have been experiencing on the upper Willamette, I almost wish now I had gotten a prop instead of a pump. The prop will give you better top end and more control when trolling in the wind. You can drop the main motor if the wind is pushing you around and it will act like a rudder. If I was in an area where I could capitalize on having a pump, perhaps I would feel differently.

Fish finder/GPS:

The fish finder or sonar is one of the most overlooked pieces of equipment on the boat. Many times I have gotten on a friend's nice new boat to find a little fish finder with a three or four inch screen with cute little fish symbols to indicate where the fish are. A word to the wise: buy a little less boat and a lot more fish finder! If all you want is something to tell you the depth so you don't run aground then one of those smaller units will serve you just fine. If you are like me and bought your boat specifically for fishing then you are going to need something a little more powerful.

The fish symbols are fine as a sales gimmick to get the unsuspecting person's attention but for actually finding fish they are very ineffective. To really be successful, you need to be able to use the manual mode in order to distinguish between air bubbles, thermo clines, downrigger balls and fish. With the unit in the automatic mode, (with the little fish swimming across the screen) everything which is suspended in the water column is registered as a fish. I highly recommend that before buying this piece of critical equipment you do a lot of shopping and research. Pay attention and don't just buy something because you feel pressured!

There are a couple of manufacturers who are at the top of the heap: Furuno, Lorance, and Humminbird. Each of these has slight variants to the general theme offered by all of them. The first thing I would recommend is to buy the best unit you can afford, you will not be sorry if you do! My second recommendation is to buy the unit with the highest pixel count and the largest screen. The larger the screen and the higher the resolution the better the picture and the easier it is to sort out the fish from the clutter.

I would also highly recommend buying a dual unit with GPS mapping capability. With a suitable lake map program installed in your unit, you get the advantage of being able to see canyons and hills underneath the surface before finding them with your downrigger weights. I also make a habit of marking my favorite trolling lines and jigging spots. This is especially helpful when you take the winter off; you can go right back to your favorite spots year after year. I have also found the ability to mark a school of fish very helpful since you can turn the boat and retrace your exact route.

GPS will also give you an accurate speed index. Since Kokanee and many other fish species are speed sensitive, requiring you to stay within specific speed parameters, this feature is extremely helpful.

When you first get your unit installed, take a day and get out on a lake with no distractions and sit down with the manual and work through the basics:

There are three critical areas in adjusting the graph.

1. Ping speed
2. Sensitivity
3. Color

The following are some recommendations based on my experience. Each unit has its own peculiarities so there will be differences in adjusting them. When I started out, it took me a couple of years to really understand how to get the most out of the unit. I hope this will help you to get ahead of the learning curve.

Turn the screen color down until it is only slightly on. You can adjust it up later.

Turn the ping speed down until the screen clutter is minimal.

Turn the sensitivity down slightly then check the screen adjusting some more until you get optimal viewing on your screen.

Try cruising around using your main motor at four or five miles per hour. When you mark fish, the arches should be distinct. The arches should be somewhat centered (meaning the arches should not angle one way or the other but be somewhat balanced). If that is off adjust the angle of the transducer up or down to make it somewhat even.

Once you get the arches showing up consistently and clearly adjust the color up slightly. The more color the more the clutter. I like a little color. Color and the shape of the arch will help you determine the difference between fish species. Kokanee are a distinct clear arch on the graph. You can have fun with this once you get it figured out and don't get too impatient because it takes years for most people to get it all together.

Next try it with your downrigger balls. They create a thick black line with turbulence so you will inevitably get yellow or turbulence around the balls. Adjust your sensitivity and color down slightly to adjust for this if it bothers you. Warmer water will mean more turbulence.

Thermo clines will show up better without the balls down, at least in my experience. Once you find the thermo cline, put your downrigger balls at that level and leave them there. There will be turbulence because the ball is plowing through the water mixing the warmer water with the cooler water.

Downriggers:

Downriggers first came into play in the early 1900's on the Great Lakes. Since that time, the principle has been consistently improved upon to get what we who use them now take for granted. One of the best fishing investments I have made was in putting downriggers on my boat. They allow me to consistently target specific depths without any guesswork as in the case of traditional trolling which relies on charts, line lengths, line weights and in-line weights. When a fish strikes my lure, I can then play that fish without all of the in-line hardware traditional trolling requires.

Another cool feature is stacking. I can stack lines on the downrigger allowing me to fish four lines off two downriggers at the same time covering four different depths with four different lures or baits. If that wasn't enough, I can add an additional lure halfway down each line giving me four more levels covered with four more baits for a total of eight different baits in the water at eight different levels.

When I got my first downriggers, two of us (a buddy and I) could target fish at specific depths; one watching the sonar and one driving the boat. The one watching the sonar would raise and lower the weights to match fish coming across the screen of the sonar. It seemed like every time we crossed through a school of fish, we ended up with at least one fish and quite often two. We thought we had

Penn manual downrigger

died and gone to heaven, the fishing was so easy! In my friends eyes I had mastered the fishing science and I could walk on water. In truth, that was only the beginning. When we tried out the downriggers, we were in the middle of a hot bite and when that happens, it seems you can seemingly do no wrong. Since those days, I have since had many years of humbling experiences and fishless days to keep my swelling head under control. During the course of time, I have also been able to learn the ins and outs of downriggers and downrigger practices. There are two types of downriggers; manual and electric. Each has its benefits and also its downside. Depending on your budget, you can get into a good set of downriggers for as little as a couple hundred dollars. You can also spend way in excess of $3000.00 if you are so inclined. Having always been on a fairly tight budget, I started out as inexpensively as I could while still recognizing quality. A friend of mine bought a set (prior to my finding some) that had masts on them the size of a large pencil. One weight hung up on the bottom and the downrigger was toast, mast broken, or at least twisted and he was spending another seventy five bucks to replace the damaged one. With that in mind, I started looking for a downrigger which was *Kent* proof (If that is possible!). I settled on a pair of Penn 600 manual downriggers I found on EBay. I only had a limited amount to spend and because of that, when bidding I always factored in the total cost including shipping. I lost a few auctions before I finally won what would become a life changing experience. The Penn's are built solid and fairly foolproof. The mast is heavy and the drag is readily accessible and easily adjustable. I paid less than a quarter of the cost of a new set and ended up with units which served me well for several years. Should you go down the road of buying used, do your homework! Know what you are buying beforehand by looking at the new product and checking out the way they are put

Scotty downrigger in action

together. Make sure they will handle weight in excess of ten pounds should you choose to go that route. You don't need to use weights that heavy normally but if needed it is nice to be able to do so (such as fishing deep for Chinook salmon). Make sure the mast is heavy enough just in case your weight becomes snagged (and it will on occasion!) it won't rip off the boat or bend under load. Check to make sure the drag, especially on a manual unit is easy to access and operate, if it isn't you could possibly damage your equipment and/or tip over or swamp the boat (It happens, sometimes so fast you are in the water before you realize what happened!).

Manuals are great, but they have their down fall. The first is that you have to crank up the weight every time you change your bait or get a fish on. One of the biggest downfalls for me was stacking. When letting down the weight in deep water, sometimes the line doesn't pay out as smoothly as needed and pulls from the clip; leaving you to reel in both lines and crank up the downrigger weight to start all over again (it inevitably happens a second time to really get the blood boiling). The next pet peeve about manuals is when you are in tight conditions (trolling close to either a bank or other boats) and you come up on a ridge or submerged hill. You have to crank up the cable on both downriggers before they become hung up all while trying to keep from getting in a wreck.

Electric downriggers are in this case the best thing since sliced bread. The problems mentioned above are, (for the most part) nonexistent providing you choose well when selecting your downriggers. Once again, downriggers are not all created equal; each has good traits and bad traits. One of the worst traits of many downriggers would be the lack of service facilities here on the west coast. There are only two brands which I would recommend strictly for that reason; Cannon and Scotty. The other brands are, for the most part, well made and will be more than adequate but if they go down, you end up shipping them to the East coast for service and of course this will happen right when the fish are really biting! Because of that, I will focus on these two makers. I currently have Scotties mounted on my boat and for my situation, they serve me well. They have all of the features I wanted in a downrigger with the exception of an automatic down setting. After using them continually now, (I normally try and fish at least three days a week) I am quite satisfied and in retrospect

Note the weight retrieval system (yellow collar and line running back to gunnels)

I am not sure the automatic down mode is necessary or even needed in my situation (I am a hopeless gadget freak!). I can think of one instance when the automatic down mode would be handy: when fishing alone it would enable you to get lines back in the water faster during a hot bite.

It is very nice to be able to clear your lines quickly when you are getting into shallow water or you have a hard fighting fish that is going to possibly get hung on the downrigger cable. When you need to raise the weights, you can reach over and either push the button and raise it a minor amount or throw the switch and bring it all the way up. When you choose to bring the weights all the way up, they stop as if by magic at the water line which is something you could never accomplish with manual downriggers when you are fighting a fish, all by yourself.

I did a survey of people who have either Cannon (*and by the way, unfortunately, I am not a member of **that** Cannon family*) or Scotty and found that the lines are drawn much like the lines between the owners of Chevy and Ford. Each has its strong points as well as weak points. The following paragraphs will roughly outline some of the differences.

Cannon's clutch is easily adjustable with a knob on the outside where Scotty has an adjustment just under the cover which requires another step when changing the drag. I have not found it to be a significant problem, but it is a consideration.

Cannon has a bottom tracking system which will adjust your weight in relation to the bottom which will, (hopefully) help to keep you from getting hung up on the bottom. The problem with this technology is that it is quite expensive and is out of reach for the more $$$ conscious.

Scotty has the lowest amp draw of the two and as such putts less demand on your battery. I like this feature because I have my sonar/GPS, auto pilot and lighting as well as a bilge pump relying on my battery power, so the less load the better. There is nothing worse than fishing 'til dark only to discover your battery is dead, although I did add another battery just for that reason!

As I pointed out earlier, Cannon has an auto down which will drop your weight to the desired depth automatically. This is a nice feature in theory, but my personal experience has been that it is too slow in the auto mode. With the Scotty's, the manual clutch for dropping your weights works well and really doesn't tie up your time or concentration and you can put your weights down as fast as you please.

The tilt up feature on the Scotty's is superior to that of the Cannon's. The tilt feature is nice when docking and on and off loading your boat. You can raise the mast or arm up and it is out of the way.

Both Cannon and Scotty have a swivel feature which allows you to turn the downrigger to allow weight installation and removal as well as store them while underway. Another nice feature both makers have is a weight storage hook. Some of the units don't come with this feature but you can add it after the fact.

When mounting your downriggers, mount them as far to the rear of the boat as is comfortable to be able to safely and easily operate them. That will help to keep the cables and your fishing lines out of the prop. Make sure the mast or arm of the downrigger is long enough to get away from the boat giving you even more clearance from the prop. Both Scotty and Cannon have units available with adjustable arms which allow you to extend up to 60 inches from the side of the boat.

One thing you should add on whether you have a Cannon, Scotty, or any other manual or electric downrigger is a weight retrieval system. When leaning over the side of the boat it is easy to slip and fall overboard which can have fatal consequences. As I stated earlier, I fish by myself a lot and in the process have had a few close calls leaning over the side to snap into the weight. Wear a life jacket!

There is quite an assortment of downrigger weights available to the downrigger fisherman. I have tried many different styles of weights over the years and I have a personal preference in that area. I prefer pancake weights over all of the other varieties I have tried to date with the exception of the pipe version. The reason for this is that they track very well (don't spin) and the thin design cuts down on drag which allows my weight to hang for the most part straight down.

LIGHTBULB MOMENT ☼: Take a piece of stainless steel pipe and fill it with lead embedding a stainless steel wire loop in the upper end. Put two heavy swivels on the loop, one for your downrigger cable and one for your clip to snap into. The long weight will give you notice when tapping the bottom while the long thin design will give negligible blow back.

My Third choice would be either eight or ten pound balls with a rudder fin. Anything less than eight pounds will have quite a bit of blow back (drag pulling the weight to the rear) when fishing at depth. They don't work as well as the pancakes in preventing spin but they are much superior to the cheaper round ball design. I have used both coated and uncoated balls over the years. I prefer the vinyl coated version. They are less apt to give off an electric charge and they are much less likely to mar anything they come in contact with.

Here are few tips and tricks I have learned over the years which may help out in keeping a downrigger fishing trip positive:

    1. First, be careful and keep your hands away from the cables, especially where they pass through pulleys.

    2. Wear gloves when handling cables if you must mess with them.

3. Have a pair of wire cutters handy by each of your downriggers in case you must get free of a bottom snagged cable.

4. Keep a couple of terminator clip kits and extra weights handy just in case you lose a weight or you get a kink in your cable. You could save a fishing trip by being prepared!

5. Check the cable terminators daily and you can save yourself lots of dollars in lost weights.

6. Spray your plug ends and sockets with silicone electrical spray to keep corrosion at bay. The terminals are close together and in a wet environment, bad things happen.

Downrigger Releases:

As with everything else, I have gone through a large variety of downrigger releases, usually due to operator error and/or weight terminal failure. You ask any five different Kokanee fishermen and you will get five different opinions on who makes the best release. I have my favorites just like everyone else so rather than belabor the point I will get into the pros and cons of the releases I have tried. Scotty makes a good release which just happens to be one of the first that

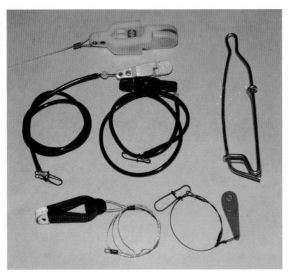

Top: Offshore light release, Middle: assorted Sep's Profishing releases, Bottom: Left Scotty release Right: Shasta Ultra release, far Right: Stacking clip

I tried many years ago. They come in a variety of sizes both stackable and otherwise. They have an adjustment which enables you some degree of control over how hard it is to pull the line from the clip.

Sep's Pro Fishing has a good release available which is adjustable by sliding the spring forward or back in the clip to adjust the release tension. These work well and in fact, are preferred by some of the people who have been a guest on my boat.

Shasta Tackle's Ultra Release is one of my personal favorites. This release requires a little more getting used to because you must first put a twist in the line before sticking it in the clip requiring two hands. The tension on the line is adjusted by a simple screw allowing easy tension adjustment for multiple sizes of line. Since there are no pads on this release, there are no wear points.

Vance's Tackle offers a good release which offers adjustment of the spring by sliding it forward or backwards for heavy or light tension similar to the Sep's version.

Another good release is offered by Offshore Tackle. Their releases are a little larger than those listed above, but are every bit as functional. They also offer replacement pads for their clips.

When using downrigger clips, you have two options; the first is to have the release set so that the instant a fish strikes it pulls from the clip. The second option is to have the release set with a little more tension so the fish stays in the clip after the strike. Both are correct and both work well under different conditions.

When you are stacking lines on a downrigger, if your release is set too stiff, the fish will inevitably get tangled in the other stacked line or in your ball troll. When stacking I like the release to allow the fish to pull out of the clip and not end up with a big wad of tangled line which is very frustrating, remember this is supposed to be fun!

When I am running one line per downrigger, I like to set the release with more tension and keep smaller fish in the clip so I can release them manually. The reason for this is that when fishing deep, there is a lot of slack line if the fish quickly releases from the clip. When I manually release from the clip, I have the opportunity to take up slack line before the fish can throw the hook. You can make your own observations with those two things in mind; after all it is all a matter of personal perspective.

LIGHTBULB MOMENT ☼_:_ If when you have the standard clip type such as with Scotty, Sep's and Vance's, and you cannot get the tension needed to keep your line in the clip by adjusting the spring, just put a couple of twists in the line before clipping the resulting loop into the jaws of the clip. That will give some added tension and help to keep the line in the clip jaws.

Auto Pilot:

TR-1 Gold Autopilot

This is one of the neatest add-on products I have come across over the years. For the avid fisherman who spends lots of time fishing alone this product is almost a must! The TR-1 Gold, produced and sold by Garmin, is a simple autopilot system mounted on the trolling motor with a small computer mounted near the rear of the boat and a gyro compass mounted near the front. This system will maintain a constant heading leaving you to tend your lines and reel in fish without drifting off course while your attention is elsewhere.

You can even link the unit to your GPS although I have not taken advantage of this feature. The unit comes with some built in features which include micro sensitive throttle control, man over board (which will bring you right back over the spot where the last school of fish was encountered) adjustable step turns, auto zigzag (which is great for covering a lot of water while prospecting) It also has many more features which make this, in my opinion, one of the best additions to a serious fisherman's boat. I installed the unit myself, the directions were straightforward and easy to understand and I completed the installation in a couple of evenings after work. This little contraption is also a great addition to the boat which is used to target multiple northwest species. It is very effective for backtrolling in water which would be virtually impossible to fish in that fashion without it.

Electric Trolling Motors:

I would be remiss in my duties if I didn't mention electric trolling motors. This technology has come a long way due to their heavy use in bass fishing. In a lot of ways they are superior to the kicker with the TR-1 attached. Mounted on the front of your boat, they provide excellent control in the wind and have another advantage in that they are completely quiet. The better units have the ability to link up with GPS and follow a course and they will even memorize the course you take and will automatically back track over your course if you desire. They will also maintain a constant, stationary position when jigging towards shore; until you want to move further down the shore to try a new area. These units have many of the features of the TR-1 plus the advantage of holding in one area. The cost, less thc required batteries is somewhat lower than that of the TR-1, but when you add in the batteries the cost starts getting up there, especially if you go with the more stable gel batteries. In any event, this is one item you should have on your want list for your next birthday or maybe Christmas.

Nets:

There are now quite a few nets on the market with a focus on the Kokanee fishery. Many like the nets with the long handles because

Kokanee go berserk when they see the boat. Others like the shorter

EGO S2 Slider REACH Large PVC coated mesh landing net

nets because they are easier to handle when fishing alone. No matter what length of handle you prefer, if you are buying new, get a net which features a rubber or non-snagging net. That will save you an immense amount of grief when landing fish. The old style nylon nets seemed to attract hooks and you spend so much time getting your lines back in the water after fighting that style of netting it is worth extra money just to avoid that calamity not to mention the rubber nets are less intrusive to non target fish you wish to release unharmed.

Another nice feature is a floating net. If you are out on the lake and you inadvertently lose the net over the side, it will slip from view to never be seen again just out of your reach. That creates a problem since most of us don't carry a spare. There are several good landing nets out there: Ego, Frabill and Ranger just to name a few. I believe Ego is the only one of the group which floats although I am sure that will change.

Thermometers:

My thermometer rigged with chain swivel and 3 OZ weight ready to clip on the downrigger cable

One of those is a good water temperature gauge. I bought mine off the shelf at a local sporting goods store in the fly fishing equipment. This thermometer made by Vexilar is my second in several years and can be found for fewer than ten bucks. It has a depth gauge on it which I have never used. The only thing I like to occasionally check is the temperature at depth. Fitted on a bead chain with a duo snap and a 3 Oz weight I can clip it on the downrigger cable and let it fall all the way down to the ball. Next time I raise the ball, I just check the temperature at the depth I have been fishing. Since 55 degrees is the center line of preferred temperature, I shoot for my downrigger offerings to be within about a ten foot margin. There are also fancy electronic sensors which are available which will give forward speed at depth and water temperature. No matter what your preference is, there is something out there to scratch your itch, and lighten your wallet.

Black Box:

Black Boxes are another item which are/were promoted for the inland downrigger fisherman. I have never used one, but I have done quite a bit of research on them. Since my boat is welded aluminum, I was at first quite concerned about the negative effects of electric current being released into the water from my boat. To date, I have not had any negative effects from this problem. I suspect that as my boat ages and bad wiring comes into play this may become more of an issue. Cannon has the technology built right into their higher end line of downriggers which is a nice feature. Both Scotty, Pro-Troll and a few others offer their own versions of this black box technology starting at around $110.00. The long and the short of it is, fish are attracted to positive electrical charge and repelled by a negative charge. Each boat is different both in fresh and in salt water. One thing to help eliminate or at least keep this minimized is to maintain the sacrificial metals on both your boat and outboard motors. A simple brushing with a brass or stainless steel brush will keep the surface clean and give you the optimum exchange. If your sacrificial anodes are in good shape and you have no frayed wires leaking current into the water, the positive voltage will actually attract fish as well as prevent corrosion of the metal parts of your boat in contact with the water. If a boat is set up properly all of the electrolysis is dissipated harmlessly in the zinc sacrificial anodes. As this happens, it creates a positive field around your boat which can attract fish. If you are interested in further researching this phenomenon you can look up Pro-Troll's website and either purchase the book or browse through the troubleshooting portion of their website. Typical metals used as sacrificial anodes on boats include aluminum, copper, steel, brass, stainless steel and zinc.

Ron Walker on left and Chester Jahn on the right with a pair of awesome Kokanee caught out of Wallowa Lake.
Photo Courtesy of Jeremy Jahn

3 ...The Rod & Reel, the Terminal Tackle and the Bait

Finally, a chapter on the real hardware that puts the fish in the boat! The following pages will take you on a journey through the many types and manufacturers of terminal gear for Kokanee. Most people don't think of the terminal gear starting with rod and reel but in this case, it does. Kokanee present a unique situation both with their soft mouth and their extreme effort to be free of the hook; thrashing, rolling and doing tail walks much like a Steelhead only in a smaller body. In the

following pages I will take you through the many advances which have been made in recent years in rod, reel, terminal tackle and bait.

Rods & Reels:

Rod and reel combinations vary depending on the type of fishing you are going to be doing; for example a rod and reel combination which is good for trolling will not work well for jigging and vise versa. The trolling rod is too limber for a good hook set and the reel won't get the jig to depth fast enough.

On the other hand, the jigging rod is too stiff for trolling and can result in lost fish. The jigging reel will lead to lots of line twist and lost fishing time due to tangled lines. The lines used for jigging will end up costing you fish due to the lack of line stretch, while the lines used for trolling will cause you to miss strikes because of line stretch.

Trolling Rods:

Trolling rods should have less backbone and act as a shock absorber when a fish strikes the lure. The jigging rod needs to have backbone for lightning fast hook sets. Picture a railroad car moving along at 1.2 MPH. You reach out and grab the car from a stationary position. Which is going to be influenced, the railroad car or you? Your grabbing of the railroad car caused not even a minute difference in the forward motion of the car. Instead, the car would cause you to follow so long as you hang onto the car. That is what it is like for a fish grabbing the lure at the end of your line. Your boat doesn't hesitate, even for one instance. Instead the fish is dragged along much against its wishes, thrashing and fighting against the sudden change of direction. Add to that the soft mouth of the fish and you have created a situation requiring some sort of shock absorption. The shock absorption in this case is twofold, first you have the rod with an amazing amount of flex clear down to the reel seat and secondly you have monofilament line which can have up to 30% stretch. With the soft mouth of the Kokanee and the wild frantic fight of this fish, you want a rod and line which will continue to give shock absorption right up to the moment you land the fish.

Most of the earlier Kokanee trolling rods were either custom made or were rods made out of fiberglass meant for other purposes. Kokanee trolling rods available today over the counter are 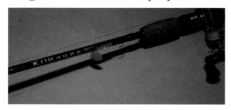 predominantly made out of the traditional fiberglass as opposed the graphite rods which have become so popular for salmon and trout rods, primarily due to the forgiving action of the fiberglass rod. As mentioned earlier, a good downrigger trolling rod must be forgiving. In addition, the rod must also be able to handle larger fish and keep you in control, not the other way around. During the course of writing this book, I have reviewed several rods by various manufacturers specifically designed for Kokanee fishing. Each good downrigger rod has unique features which set it apart from the rods of their competitors. Those features will determine for you which rod is right for you as an individual. No two fishermen have the same opinion as to the best rod for the situations encountered but hopefully I can give you some direction here which will help in your quest for the best rod.

The last three or four years have seen some major improvements and availability of rods specifically for the Kokanee fisherman. All of the major manufacturers now offer decent rods for Kokanee trolling, most of which are available for under $100.00. For the more discriminating fisherman, there are rods available into the several hundred dollar range. The rods covered in this book are all available for fewer than one hundred dollars. It has been my experience, the more a rod costs, the more likely it is going to 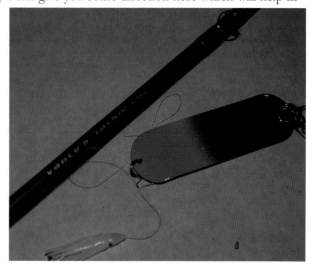 be broken by a guest on my boat (of which there have been many) and it is easier on my pocket book and blood pressure to keep less expensive rods on the boat (remember, this is supposed to be fun!).

The trolling rods which I have reviewed specifically for this book are as follows: Okuma Kokanee Pro, Lamiglas Kokanee Special, Tica Kokanee and Vance's Tackle; Spiral Wrapped Rod. All of these rods are very forgiving and in my opinion great buys. For lakes with smaller fish and not much chance of bycatch I would lean towards the Lamiglass simply because it is a US rod. The Okuma has a similar backbone and is quite a bit of fun to land fish with. The Tica is a great rod, especially for mid sized fish and will really enhance the bite. Bare in mind rods built in the US will cost more, but by buying US you are supporting our American makers. Vance's Tackle makes a rod which is slightly heavier and created on a fly rod blank. I really enjoy catching larger fish on this rod and it is my go-to rod when the bye catch of large fish such as German Browns or Mackinaw are a good possibility. I have landed larger fish on the other rods mentioned but they are a little lightweight for larger fish in my opinion.

Trolling Reels:

Reels for downrigger fishing are also a specialized item specifically set up for trolling. The most effective reel for trolling is the level wind or bait casting reel. Spinning reels put out too much line twist to be effective over an extended period of time. Line twist leads to rat's nests

and tangles which means you are spending time repairing your gear instead of fishing. A level wind reel is a traditional reel (non-spinning) with a line guide which lays your line on the spool evenly from side to side as the line is retrieved. The line spool is horizontal to the rod allowing the line to pay out directly down the rod with no line twist. Spinning reels have the line spool parallel with the rod and pay out directly off the end of the spool, twist and all. When retrieving the line with a spinning rod, you put approximately five twists in your

Tica Caiman level wind reels specifically for Kokanee

line for every crank of the reel handle which leads to lots of tangles when fishing. The body of a bait casting reel is normally made of one of two types of material: aluminum or graphite. Graphite reels are lightweight and highly resistant to corrosion, however not quite as strong or durable as aluminum.

Another important consideration when looking for a casting reel is the ball bearings or bushings inside the reel. These are the components of the reel which have the most direct impact on the smoothness and "feel" of the reel. As a general rule, stainless steel ball bearings are preferable to bushings. Usually, the more ball bearings the unit contains, the smoother the

cranking will be. Smooth cranking is essential for a good fishing reel of any type, so you can feel the action. Bait casting reels come with a range of ball bearing counts, usually from two to six. Two bearings would be an absolute minimum. The fisherman should purchase a reel with the most bearings his budget will allow. Obviously, the more bearings a reel contains, the more expensive the reel will be.

Another important feature to consider is line retrieval rate or turn ratio of the handle. Bait casting reels come with a variety of turn ratios ranging all the way to 7:1. The second number refers to the number of turns of the crank, while the first

Abu Garcia 6501C3 Ambassador a good solid reel!

number refers to the number of times the spool rotates. For example 7:1 means that for every turn of the crank the spool turns 7 times, which is obviously a very high rate of line return. One more thing to look for in a reel is that the line guide moves back and forth as the line pays out. This is a great way to keep track of how much line is paying out as well as keeping in sync with the line laid out on the reel. For example, this feature is found in the Abu Garcia but not on the Tica. Simply it is a matter of what is important to you the end user.

Jigging Rods:

When jigging, the same soft rod and line stretch encountered in the example above is not your friend. Picture your jig running down 40 feet to a school of fish. You have lowered your jig (or jig and bait in the case of bait fishing) and as you jig your line, you feel a bump from a fish on the other end. You quickly raise your rod tip to set the hook on the unsuspecting fish on the other end. In the process of raising your rod tip, the line begins to stretch, if the line stretches to the 30 percent as mentioned above, you will have to raise the rod tip twelve feet before the jig at the end of you line moves an inch. Because of this, braided low-stretch lines have become the norm for jigging along with stiffer rods with sensitive tips (so you can detect slight bites or strikes) for lightning fast hook sets.

Jigging rods are vastly different from the downrigger rod. These rods are made out of different materials and have a totally different action than that of the downrigger rod. Jigging rods are much stiffer, preferably having a medium/fast action. Unlike the downrigger rod which is a shock absorber, the jigging rod is designed to give immediate action as opposed to the soft cushioning action of the downrigger rod. The good jigging rod is usually made out of graphite and has a good backbone and fast action at the tip. When jigging it is the jigger who sets the hook as opposed to trolling where the forward motion of the boat does the work. When jigging, you are usually fishing in from four to 110 feet of water. The methods used to target this range of water are similar. Jigging is the process of alternately retrieving a lure and letting it fall. The lure flutters as it is falling and attracts the strike. Because of the technique, the strike will often be subtle and brief which requires a fast hook set. Rods which will work well for this type of fishing can vary between one designed for long casts and rods which are designed for vertical fishing. One rod can and will work for both although if you are like me, I have a rod for every conceivable circumstance. I like a longer rod for casting, possibly from my background of growing up in the northwest and targeting Steelhead. I prefer a shorter rod for jigging vertically because I don't want to deal with the extra rod length when landing fish in that fashion. Regardless of your rod length preference, the action of the rod is the same; medium/fast. When jigging being able to immediately sense the strike or bump is of the utmost importance! You only get one chance for the hookset and missed hook sets mean less fish in the boat.

For clarity, I will attempt to distinguish between horizontal jigging and vertical jigging. Horizontal jigging can be as simple as casting a lure or jig out, letting it fall (depending on the depth), retrieving it a short distance and repeating the procedure. Vertical jigging consists of letting your lure out to a given depth and raising the rod and letting the jig or lure fall a short distance while feeling for the bite. In both cases, the fish usually strikes on the fall. Being able to see or feel the strike is very important in both cases. Due to the fact Kokanee are aggression biters defending personal space, the strikes are usually sudden and brief as opposed to the strike of a predatory fish which is biting to fill its stomach. Because of this, when a Kokanee strikes it does not typically inhale a lure or jig but only bumps it. A brown trout on the other hand will inhale a smaller lure with gusto. The hook set on the brown might not be needed while a hook set on a Kokanee is required ninety nine percent of the time when jigging due to the difference in the strike.

Drop shot rods developed for bass fishing are proving to be very effective rods for jigging due to the sensitivity of the rod and similarity of the technique. Early on, at least here in the USA, the technique was considered a deep water technique but has now evolved to a distance (casting) technique as well. The rods developed for this technique are proving to be just as effective when used for Kokanee jigging. The cost of these rods runs anywhere from $50.00 up through $500.00 plus. You can get by with any rod with a medium action and good tip sensitivity. There are rods available which will suit almost anyone's budget. The main point here is that you buy the best equipment your budget will allow! You don't have to go out and spend copious amounts of cash to get results and quite honestly, for most people, a moderately priced rod will not make you cry when it inevitably gets broken by someone stepping on it.

Jigging Reels:

The better reels for jigging are spinning reels. Spinning reels enable the jigger to get the bait into the strike zone faster than the traditional casting reel. The biggest single factor in picking out a good spinning reel is the amount of ball bearings that are in the drive mechanism (which is where the handle is turned). Just as with casting reels, the more ball bearings, the better the reel. The fewer ball bearings there are, the more play or slop there is in the handle, and the less play there is, the better the reel. Some manufactures who produce quality spinning reels would include: Abu Garcia, Daiwa, Pflueger, Quantum, and Shimano.

When jigging, most use braided lines, so when selecting a reel, select one that will handle braided line. The newer reels made specifically for braid will have fewer hiccups in the way of rat's nests and tangles which will lead to less frustration and a more enjoyable fishing experience.

Lake Troll Assortment. Top: Vance's Tackle, 2nd from top: Luhr Jensen, 3rd from top: Sep's Pro Fishing, Bottom: Mack's Lure (the white spacers were needed to photograph the flashers)

Flashers:

Flashers, not to be confused with dodgers, usually consist of a series of blades of various sizes which are run inline generally right in front of the lure or bait of choice. Flashers have been around for years and are or were in fact, the original lake trolling device of choice for attracting a strike. Names like Cowbell, Beer Can and Ford Fender have been ingrained into the fisherman's mind. The simple truth is that these devices work.

The main drawback to using lake trolls or flashers is the excessive drag they produce, robbing the fisherman of the joy of feeling a fighting fish on the end of their line. In the case of

Kokanee, there had to be further modifications to allow for the soft mouth of the quarry in the form of rubber snubbers. Many modifications have been made to the original flasher technology by reducing the size and weight so the fisherman can enjoy more of the thrill of landing a fish as opposed to feeling like you are reeling in a boot. I still remember my first experience trolling at a very young age. The rods were heavy, level wind reels, and the weight of the lake trolls, in this case Ford Fenders, followed by a Mack's Wedding Ring spinner tipped with corn and a portion of worm or Pautzke's egg. It was exciting catching fish, and we caught a lot of them but it was not nearly as fun as catching a fish on just a spinner or even still bait fishing where you could feel and enjoy the fight on a light rod and reel.

Companies like Mack's Lure, Sep's Pro Troll, Shasta Tackle, and Vance's Tackle have all come out with their own versions of this traditional piece of gear. There is a wide variety of light weight flasher systems available to the angler who does not want to drag around all of the hardware of yesterday. I have recently tried out several new versions and at first I had reservations about even putting them in this book due to the issues already mentioned. I am happy to report that you can now land fish on light tackle using light weight flashers and still enjoy the fight of the fish on the end of your line. Furthermore, light weight lake trolls enable the beginning Kokanee fisherman the opportunity to target a fish otherwise inaccessible. The first thing to note about most light weight flashers is that there is a front and a back. The front end usually has a rudder (either plastic or stainless steel) or a three way spreader. In the case of the rudder, there is sometimes a small hole where a weight can be attached to achieve greater depth. The spreader bar serves the same purpose, only without the stabilizing blade. The other end of the troll or flasher will have a swivel onto which is clipped the leader leading to the lure or spinner of choice.

The blades of the flasher are designed to roll, catching the light penetrating the water giving off flash which in turn simulates a school of fish, attracting other fish and inciting a reaction. The lure selected to follow the flashers needs to have some action of its own. A few good choices would be: a spinner, spoon or a hoochie with a device such as a smile blade or wiggle hoochie to give it action. Note: a hoochie without some sort of action producing device will seldom do well in this situation. Since the lure of choice has an action of its own, be sure to run a minimum of twenty four inches or more of leader behind the lake troll to allow the lure to work properly and achieve its best action.

Ball Trolls:

Ball Trolls from the left: Vance's Tackle, Sep's Profishing

Ball trolls are the answer to the guy who is fishing with downriggers to avoid the drag created by fishing with traditional lake trolls. My first ball trolls were simply lake trolls attached to a large ball bearing swivel clipped to my downrigger ball. To be quite honest, the lake troll version worked very well as long as I was careful to not drop the weights too fast causing the line stacked above, to get tangled up in the ball troll.

Once the sun is high in the sky and the summer fishing season is in full swing, ball trolls are my go-to attractor. Kokanee are attracted to flash and ball trolls can and will improve your catch rate. When I first started using ball trolls, I ran the downrigger release off the rear of the troll which impeded the action of the troll. Once the line was loaded by either the line drag in the water or by putting a load on the rod, the end of the lake troll or, in this case the ball troll, the trailing end was raised which killed most or all of the action of the blades. Once while dropping the weight, I was watching the troll as it dropped out of site with tension on the line causing the troll to arch towards the surface thereby killing the action. I quickly brought the weight back up and added a stacker clip for the line about three feet up and again watched as the weight went down. The flashers blades were all working well now; uninhibited by the tension on the line.

Today, there are several high quality ball trolls made specifically for the downrigger fisherman, companies like: Crystal Basin, Sep's Pro Fishing, and Vance's Tackle all put out a very high quality product. Ball trolls are designed to be run directly off the ball, in place of the release which normally would be located there. In order to properly use the ball troll and not inhibit its fish attracting properties, a stack-able line release should be located anywhere from three to five feet above the troll. The tip of your lure following a dodger should be no more than twelve feet behind the downrigger cable. To go more, you greatly reduce the attraction of the ball troll to your presentation. One of the big benefits of running your line this close to the cable is that tight turns are easy to make without getting your lines tangled up in the cables as is the case when running line out twenty feet or more. It has long been taught by experienced Kokanee fishermen that as the season progresses, the dodger gets larger. The reasoning for this is simple. The fish get more aggressive as they get closer to spawning. Larger dodgers mean more drag on your line. I have found the flat blades of the largest Shasta Sling Blade tend to minimize the drag (when running larger dodgers) but nothing like a ball troll with your line stacked above running a small dodger or even none at all. For me, it has always been about minimal tackle and the joy of the fight so in this case, I can have the flash and attraction without the detraction and drag of the heavier gear.

Dodgers:

Dodgers are a single blade with one or two bends designed to create flash (which attracts fish) and vibration. Dodgers do not roll; they dodge back and forth, hence the name dodger. If you are trolling too fast for the dodger you are using, it will start to roll and lose its primary attraction. Dodgers come in multiple sizes, shapes, metals and colors each of which has a time and a place where it will work the best. Due to the large variety of dodgers on the market, with each manufacturer promoting their dodger as the go-to unit, there has developed following similar to that of the car makers Ford and Chevrolet.

The truth is each of them has their pros and cons and because of that I recommend you carry a selection in your tackle box. Depending on the speed at which you troll, you will need to choose a dodger designed for that speed. Less bend allows faster speeds without spinning while more bend gives better action at slow speeds. My recommendation is to have a

Assorted Dodgers from top: (2) Vance's Tackle,
2nd Row Lft: Sep's Pro Fishing, Rt: Mack's Lure,
3rd row (3) Crystal Basin,
4th row: (2) Shasta Sling Blade

selection of offerings by various manufacturers because each has strong points in different situations. Crystal Basin, Father Murphy, Shasta Tackle, Vance's, Sep's Pro Fishing and Mack's Lure all offer a different type of dodger which fit specific conditions. Other things to consider in addition to trolling speed are the hardware, bend and finish attached to the dodger. The bend in the dodger determines the amount of thump or sound (vibration) the dodger transmits to attract fish. The higher quality the finish, the longer the dodger will last, providing you don't lose it to a submerged stump or ledge. The hardware attached to the dodger in the form of rings, swivels and snaps are also important.

The rings are important because it is a real pain when your line gets caught in the split ring of the dodger. Not only does it screw up the action, it has the potential to cut or wear your line. You can get around this by adding some JB Weld® to the rings to keep the line from becoming caught in the split. The snaps and swivels are important because if your gear becomes caught on a submerged log or rock, something has to give, and you could lose your entire terminal setup instead of just the gear at the end. It is very disconcerting to reel in your line and have the remains of a snap swivel and nothing else after crossing an underwater ridge or other submerged structure. Quality swivels and snaps help to prevent those unfortunate incidents. Every one of these quality touches add value to the dodger and increase the cost as well.

Cross Section of Original Blade

Cross Section of Single Bend Modifacation

Cross Section of Double Bend Modifacation

Examples of bending Shasta Sling Blade, Father Murphy, and RMT dodgers to achieve good action when trolling slowly.

When fishing with dodgers, be aware of the different types of fish inhabiting the lake. Many times Kokanee are the main forage for larger predators such as Mackinaw and Chinook. Larger fish will shadow the schools of Kokanee looking for their next meal. Because of this, Kokanee can be overly sensitive to excessive flash and the thump of a dodger. Dodgers with a slight bend and less flash will sometimes be more effective where the fish are gun shy of larger predators. The color and flash of dodgers can make or break your day. Don't hesitate to change out your dodgers just like you would lures when not getting bites. I try to keep dodgers with varying degrees of thump as well as different metals and finishes specifically for those days when nothing seems to be working.

Spoons:

Spoons come in all shapes, sizes and materials and are probably one of the most underutilized lures of all the Kokanee tackle available on the market today. Apex, Dick Nite, Father Murphy, Pro-Troll, Shasta, Sep's, and Vance's Tackle all provide quality spoons which work extremely well in pursuit of Kokanee.

When fished behind a dodger or flashers, I prefer to run between 24 and 30 inches of leader giving the spoon the

Sep's Profishing: Kokanee Kandy

ability to flutter or move as it was designed to. Most Spoons can be effective at almost any speed commonly used for targeting Kokanee. Some spoons such as the Apex or the Kokanee Killer will start to roll when fished too fast. Bearing this in mind, always make a habit of running the lure and dodger alongside the boat to make sure you are getting the optimum action at the speed you are fishing. You can easily vary your speed while checking the action. I have effectively trolled spoons (depending on type) from .5 Mph up to 2.1 Mph. Every situation is different and can change by the day or the body of water you are fishing. Small spoons work

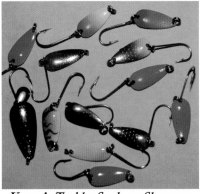

Vance's Tackle: Sockeye Slammer

exceptionally well when the fish are gun shy as in the case of heavy predation by other species. The finishes available for spoons today are exceptional in that we now have both UV finishes and glow finishes. In the case of the metal spoons the glow particles are encased in the paint while in the case of plastic spoons such as the Apex, the glow particles are encased in the plastic of the lure giving it more durability for those, who like myself, are guilty of being hard on equipment. When fishing the UV products, I try to pay attention to the UV index which is

Assorted Apex spoons by Hot-Spot

available on several weather related sources over the internet. When using the glow products, you must first charge the lure by one of several methods. In the early morning before strong daylight you can charge the lures with a camera flash or a charging box which will charge several items including dodgers at the same time. This box can be constructed out of plywood and utilize a 12 volt black light which can be plugged in to the ACC of your boat. During the day, you can set your glow lures and dodgers on a piece of foil or a foil covered piece of plywood for a few minutes before putting them in the water. Most of

the products I have tested so far do better when charged every fifteen minutes or so although some will retain their charge for up to six hours. This is not a bad thing and can actually help by getting you in the habit of changing out your gear on a regular basis.

Spin offs are one of the common problems which are often experienced when using spoons. Apex has gotten around this by having the line slide through the lure with dual hooks. When the fish hits and inevitably rolls up in your line, the lure slides up the line not allowing the fish leverage to throw or pull the hook out. Not so with the traditional spoons, with only one hook available they have more

Shasta Tackle: Hum Dingers in the center and Cripplure on the perimeter

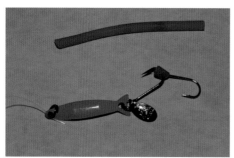

Example of adding an extra hook to a spoon using a portion of snubber or surgical tubing

chance of throwing the hook. One simple method of dealing with this is to use ¼ or 1/8" surgical tubing and a second hook which opposes the first hook (see photo). Take a second hook (preferably a thin wire hook) and slip a short piece of surgical tubing over the eye of the hook. Next slide the point of the hook attached to the lure through the surgical tubing and the eye of the second hook. The surgical tubing keeps the second hook from sliding off the first hook and at the same time gives you the opportunity to hook the fish a second time preventing spin offs. I have also tried changing out the hooks on my most effective lures. Most lures are made using open eye Siwash hooks in order to stay competitively priced. My hooks of choice are thin wire sickle hooks. The only tools it takes to change out the hooks are a pair of snap ring pliers and the hooks of choice. I have also found that by exchanging the hooks provided by the lure maker for lighter higher quality thin wire hooks, the action of the lure is increased due to less weight on the back of the spoon.

When buying spoons, look for glow colors first and UV colors second. Glow will work in almost all conditions while UV will only be effective when UV rays are available (check the UV index). I also like a selection of brass, gold and silver plate in both hammered and smooth finish. These lures will work when nothing else will, you just have to give them time on the end of your line to find out.

Spinners:

Mack's Lure: Wedding Ring Spinner

Who hasn't heard of the Wedding Ring spinner? Probably the most produced lure available on the market today in one shape or another. My first introduction to trolling was with a wedding ring spinner produced by Mack's Lures. Over the years, I have used both the original and variations of the original in a wide variety of trolling situations and conditions. I always watched for them to come on sale, buying as many as my budget would allow. Once I got into seriously pursuing Kokanee, I got into the habit of cutting off and throwing away the single heavy hook and replacing it with either double Gamakatsu octopus hooks or double drop shot hooks. Today, wedding rings are now available with the double hooks right out of the package.

With the popularity of the wedding ring came a wealth of spinners from a large variety of Kokanee tackle producers including but not limited to: Crystal Basin, Shasta Tackle, Sep's, Mack's, R&K, and Uncle

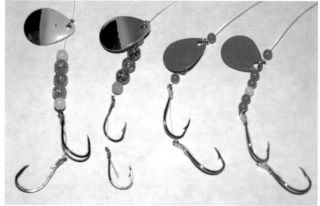

From the Left: Crystal Basin; 1 & 2, Shasta Tackle; 3 & 4

Larry's. All of these producers make exceptional products and all of them produce great results at putting fish in the cooler (see photos). If the spinner has heavy double hooks, by all means change them out with some thin wire hooks such as the Gamakatsu #4's.

For me, spinners offer a favorite means of putting fish in your boat. They come in a great variety and combination of colors which will constantly produce fish. All you have to do is pay attention to the bite and switch colors when the bite dies off. Most spinners come in UV and Glow and combinations of the two in as many colors as you have imagination. In the early days, I always tried to fish them without a dodger until I no longer caught fish which is something I sometimes forget to do nowadays. With less gear between you and the fish, the more fun the fight and the less opportunity for the fish to throw the hook. When that method no longer catches fish, I start using a dodger. Spinners can be fished with as little as eight

Shasta Tackle: PPK spinner/hoochie

inches of leader all the way up to six feet of leader. It all depends on the lake and the mood of the fish that day. I have been told by some the only way to get fish to bite a spinner is to run it short, but in truth, I have caught many fish with three or more feet of leader to the spinner. Spinners have the advantage of blade action (noise) and visual attraction (Glow & UV) to bring out the attack mode in Kokanee. Follow up with suitable bait on the trailing hooks to direct the tail biting strike of the Kokanee and you have a winning combination!

When fishing a spinner, I like to try a longer leader and shorten it up until I get the action I am looking for. It has been my experience that some lakes work better with long leaders and some with short leaders. I am unsure as to why, other than the predation issue which I brought up earlier. It is my opinion as I stated earlier, Kokanee are tail biters! They wait until the larger fish is exiting the neighborhood and shoot in for the tail nip before streaking off to safety. Picture a small (yapper) dog waiting for the bigger slow moving dog to get half way out the door before rushing in and biting or nipping at the rear of the departing larger dog. By presenting this type of stimulus you will catch more fish on lakes which hold larger predatory fish.

I like to start out running as many different color combinations as I have lines in the boat. By running all the colors I can, I will quickly find the color which is hot at the moment. I also alternate the depths of each presentation so every level in the target zone is covered. As soon as a hot color is found, I will switch over one more line to be sure before switching the rest. Once that color cools, I go back to the rotation of color until once again I find what is hot and the process starts over again. During this process, I like to mix size as well as color since sometimes larger presentations will go without interest and vise versa.

Mack's Tackle: Wedding Ring Classic, Wedding Ring Pro and Smile Blade Flies

Hoochies or Mini Squids:

R&K Pearl and Pink Hoochie

 This bait, which has been used for targeting bass, crappie and other warm water fish for years, is now being effectively used for targeting Kokanee. Several years ago I heard people were having good success using this type of bait. While tying up some spinners, I went ahead and tied up some hoochies in a couple of colors for use on one of my fishing trips. I tied up a couple dozen thinking that if they worked, I had added a whole new dimension to my Kokanee tackle box. I tried them while on that trip with little or no success. I hadn't had a lot of confidence in them to begin with and so they got retired to my tackle box for a couple more years. In the course of a conversation with another Kokanee fisherman, I found out he had been using hoochies with very good success. He went on to tell me how he was rigging them up. I went out the next day and used those hoochies which I had retired to the tackle box with pretty good success.

The trick was that I was running a longer leader of twenty inches behind the dodger when I first used them. Once I cut back the leader to between eight and twelve inches allowing the dodger to swing the bait back and forth in an inviting action, the bite turned on and I had a new and effective bait to use. With the UV and Glow configurations in a multitude of colors available, you can easily cover every color in the rainbow. Add to that

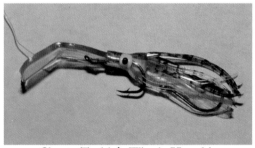

Shasta Tackle's Wiggle Hoochie

the action of a Mack's Smile blade, the wiggle of a Hoochie Thing from Crystal Basin or the Wiggle Hoochie from Shasta Tackle and you have versatile new bait with its own action. For the economy minded, you can purchase the tubes from a variety of sources and tie your own. As I stated earlier, I tied up a bunch and the beauty is they are fairly inexpensive to put out so you can fish more colors than you could initially use when relying on spinners and lures at a substantially lower cost. Not only are they easy to make, they are easy to store. I pick up a couple of plastic storage boxes at one of the home improvement centers and while I am there I buy pipe insulation which comes in six feet pieces. I then cut the insulation into lengths which fit nicely into the boxes and wrap the hoochies around the foam cylinders giving me massive storage for all of my lures.

Crystal Basin: Hoochie Thing

For those who aren't crafty or just plain don't enjoy tying their own hoochies, there are quality pre-tied hoochies or squids available from a large group of makers including: Crystal Basin, Mack's, Shasta Tackle, R&K Spinners, and Vance's. All of these companies put out a quality product at a fair price and all are tied with quality hooks and leader.

As I mentioned earlier, I started fishing these baits with a short leader which really paid off. The one exception to this is when fishing a Hoochie with an action of its own. Three good examples of this are the three baits mentioned at the beginning of this section. All three have action and added attraction of their own. I like to fish these no closer than twenty four inches behind the dodger. If the fishing is good, as it often is in the early morning, I like to run any one of these baits without a dodger so I can experience the fight of the fish mano a mano. When they stop hitting the plain bait, I will add a dodger in the smallest size I have and as the day progresses, I will move to a larger dodger still, to keep on the bite. Use a glow box or a flash to charge the hoochies when good sunlight is not available. It only takes a few minutes to charge them up and you are back in business. I will usually have several charged up and ready to go so I don't have to have my line out of the water for any period of time. I just reel in, snap in a pre-baited hoochie and back in the water it goes. When starting out, or prospecting for the colors which are going to stimulate the bite, I will run a different color for each rod in the boat just like when I am fishing spinners or spoons. Once you develop a hot color switch one other rod over and make sure before switching all of the rods. When the bite dies off, start rotating through the colors again at various depths until you find the next hot set up and the process begins anew.

Plugs:

Years ago, I read an article about Phil Johnson in which he raved over the Wee Tad which is a one piece plug which the line slides through, coming out the bottom rear of the plug to a double hook set up. I searched for years before finding that they were produced by a company in Canada by the name of Tomic Lures. There are two holes to choose from when rigging up this plug which will give you two distinctly different actions. I prefer the lower of the two hole arrangements, but in reality it is a matter of personal preference and what is working at the time. These plugs are now produced by Crystal Basin Tackle here in the US of A. Another effective plug on the market is Worden's Flat Fish. The smaller flat fish has always been a top producing trout lure, but it is also very effective for targeting Kokanee. These plugs are available in a UV version and a number of different

Crystal Basin's Wee Thing. Note how the line can slide through the plug helping to avoiding spin offs

colors which are very effective. There are a multitude of smaller plugs which can be used very effectively for targeting Kokanee.

Jigs:

Jigs come in a multitude of sizes and colors, with many different shapes and actions. Some of the more popular makes are: Luhr Jensen, Buzz Bomb, Gibbs, Acme, and Wigston Lures. To be an effective jigger, you will need an assortment of sizes (weight), color and makes. For horizontal jigging, there is also the option of using a spoon such as the Kastmaster in place of a traditional jig.

Horizontal Jigging Spoons Row 1, Tasmanian Devils (Wigston Lures) Row 2 Krocodile (Luhr Jensen) Kastmaster (Acme)

With the advent of UV and Glow finishes, you can now find your favorite jigs in both UV and Glow and combinations thereof. When fishing with jigs, it is very similar to fishing with any other type of tackle in that you will need to go through the basic colors to find the hot color of the moment. When fishing shallow, I like to use as small a jig as possible while still being able to follow the jig down with the rod and still sense the jig on the end of my line. I will gradually increase the weight of the jig as the depth increases to keep in constant touch with

my jig which is put simply by saying; slack line means missed strikes since fish usually strike on the fall.

When jigging horizontally, I like to cast out and start out with a three count. On the count of three, I jig the lure or jig back towards me at which point, I count to three again and the process starts over. A spoon such as the KastMaster® or Thomas Buoyant® work very well for this as does the Tasmanian Devil® by Wigston Lures.

When jigging vertically, simply raising your rod and then allowing the tip to fall while keeping the slack

Assorted Jigs From Top: Long and Short Buzz Bombs, 2nd & Row 3rd from Lft: Crippled Herring large & small, 4th Row from Lft: Gibbs minnow, Aufish101 custom jig

out of your line will produce hits if you are at the correct depth with your presentation. You can make it as easy or as complicated as you want to, depending on your energy level and your situation. When fishing vertically and horizontally with jigs requires a low stretch line such as braid, which is very limp, a stiff leader of about thirty inches should be between the braid and

the jig to prevent the limp line from becoming entangled in the hooks as the jig falls. Start out by pulling out even amounts of line to reach the depth that the fish are holding at. Once you are slightly over the fish, start working your jig or making it dance while staying in constant touch both by feel and by watching the rod tip. You have to develop a feel for the bite and it can at times be very frustrating. Usually while you are anchored up in a group of other jiggers, one or two people in the group will be catching ninety percent of the fish. The key is to be patient and persistent while learning to feel or sense the fish. A slight bump either seen on the rod tip or sensed through the rod should trigger a quick upward stroke of the rod to

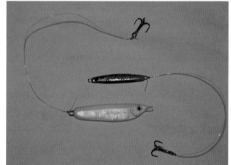

Typical modification of jig bodies for bait fishing. The shape of the jig body allows the bait to get quickly down to the fish & the stiff leader helps keep the rig from getting tangled

set the hook. You will want to reel in your catch as quickly as possible to keep the fish on the hook, usually boated without a net, just up to the surface and over the side of the boat as quickly as possible.

Jigs can also be used for still bait fishing as they are or slightly modified. When modifying, I remove the hooks from the jig and install a heavy leader in place of the original hook with a treble hook six to eight inches below the jig body. The depth is handled in much the same fashion, with the exception of the jigging part. You position the jig over the school in a stationary position and wait for the bump or dip of the rod tip which will be answered with a quick lift of the rod to set the hook. In this case, the tips of the hook are baited, usually with corn or possibly a Gulp® Maggot.

Baits:

The one bait which has been around consistently since I started fishing as a kid is corn. We used to buy a can of corn on the way to the lake and that is what we would use, sometimes in combination with worms or maggots or any number of other baits. To this day, I have caught and still continue to catch lots of fish with a simple can of shoepeg corn. The brand of choice is Jolly Green Giant. I have not found another source for this very effective bait so that is what I still use. I have tried other brands of corn but always seem to gravitate back to the old standby.

Shoepeg corn: the original Kokanee bait and it is still effective today!

A very effective bait which is available to campers spending time on the high lakes is crayfish tails. Simply put a small portion on each of the hooks.

Another option, (especially for those who live in a state where the use of corn is outlawed), is to use bay shrimp found in the meat area of the local grocery store. This bait can be further enhanced by adding both scent and dye (see below).

Today, there are several commercially produced scented baits on the market which are proving to be very effective. Fire Corn produced by Pautzke's comes in eight colors and although it is not made from shoepeg corn, it is proving to be very effective for the guy who forgets the bait at home or just doesn't want to deal with dye and scent. This corn comes with a feature which most of us who have forgotten the bait really appreciate; it has a great shelf life! Throw a few jars in the locker on your boat and it will be there for that one time when the bait is forgotten and no other bait is available.

Berkley Gulp maggots are a great bait which works well in a bunch of different circumstances. These are available in white, chartreuse, pink and natural. This bait also has a great shelf life and I use them whenever I am not getting a bite on my traditional corn baits or when I forget to bring the bait. The small maggots have an additional benefit because they are small enough not to inhibit action on the smallest of spoons!

When baiting my hooks, I always start out with the idea that small is good. I put one kernel of corn on each hook. I don't want a big blob throwing off the action of my lure of choice so I limit the amount of bait I put on the hooks. If the fish are hitting the lure instead of the hooks bringing up the rear, I will put two kernels of UV treated corn in a contrasting color to the lure on the rear hook. This will help to stop the driveby hits that seem to come when the fish is hitting the body of the lure instead of coming in from the rear.

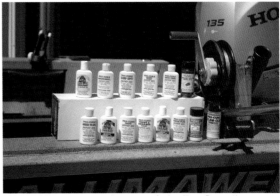

Here is a partial array of the ProCure lineup including some of their dye and powdered bait

Scents and dyes:

Scents and dyes are another part of bait preparation which can make or break the day. I religiously use both scent and dye. The new dyes that are out also have the added advantage of having a UV enhancer which when applied to your bait adds another level of attraction which has increased my catch by at least 20%. Over the years, I have tried most of the different scents on the market and I continue to experiment with various scents, dyes and gels. My first experience with scents and Kokanee fishing was with Mike's scents. I used a number of his scents including anise. After a while, I tried using Pautzke's nectar in conjunction with the Mike's scents. After doing this for several years, I tried Pro-Cure scents which came out with a UV additive in their gel. Once I tried the UV gel in a number of different formulations, I was hooked. This scent thing really works! The only drawback I found with the gel was when I was camped on a lake out in the middle of nowhere with no dishwasher it was a real pain to clean up a bunch of dodgers and lures at the end of the day. I have since graduated to the Pro-Cure line of oils. Wow, what a difference! There is little or no mess and when applied to the bait and left to marinate overnight. I came up with some fish catching potions which were unrivaled, at least in my career. By combining scents that worked well individually in varying amounts measured out with the wife's measuring spoons in the kitchen, I came up with some pretty productive mixes. I was kind of disappointed in the fact that the oils, while very effective, didn't have any flash or UV like the gels did. But, after thumbing through one of Phil Pirone's catalogs (Owner of ProCure) I saw he had a solution to my problem in the form of UV enhanced dyes and pure UV liquid. Needless to say, I have tried many winning combinations of scent and dye which work very

well. I would recommend to the person starting out with scents and dyes to try one or two scents by spitting a can into six separate zip lock baggies. Put one scent in each of three baggies and put the other scent in the other three baggies. Then put a few drops of dye in each of the baggies so you end up with three different colors of each scent. Work the corn around in the baggies so as not to crush the individual kernels, distributing the dye and the scent oil throughout the corn. Roll the bag up to force out the air from

A typical array of color based on one scent. In the spring, focus on ocean scents like krill and shrimp. In the heat of the summer run more natural lake scents

the bag and seal. Put all of the bags in the fridge overnight to marinate in the oils. Keep the corn in a small cooler handy in the back of the boat where you will be baiting up. When you are done, always return it to the cooler so the corn doesn't become mushy in the heat of the day. Pro-Cure has another product which works extremely well, "Korn Magic." This product firms up the corn when left overnight in the fridge giving you firmer kernels for cold fingers to deal with. The product also has some bite stimulating ingredients as well. When used with the oils, I have had some exceptional days on the water with long nights cleaning and packaging fish. A few of the oils that I use regularly are: Kokanee Special, Shrimp & Krill oil, Garlic Plus, Anise Plus, Carp Spit, Shrimp/Prawn and Squid oil. All of these oils and scents will help to add to your daily catch rate. Just be patient and experiment over time to develop your own favorite combinations or just use them individually.

4 ...Spring Fishing

Starting in the spring, shortly after turnover Kokanee typically move into the shallows of the lake, usually in water from four to thirty feet in depth. During this time they will target the early hatch of insects as well as larvae (see chapter one). Coming off of a semi dormant state from winter, the fish move into the shallows and feed with a vengeance. The predominant forage at this point are invertebrates such as fresh water shrimp, mayflies, damsel flies and Chironomids which are the larvae of the common midge. The best places to fish for them is around shallow points and protected shallow bays which get the most sun and have the first warm water. In these shallow points and bays you will notice lots of fish activity because of the large amount of feed available. The shallow areas will work to the angler's advantage in that fish will be concentrated while taking advantage of the readily available food. There are a number of different methods which are very effective at this time of the year including jigging, still bait fishing and trolling. Jigging and bait fishing require a little less specialized gear in the way of boats. A smaller boat works well for this technique and can be as simple as a drift boat or a small rowboat. Trolling requires more specialized gear including a trolling motor and probably downriggers as the season progresses.

Horizontal Jigging:

Probably my favorite method for catching fish at this time of year is horizontal jigging. Very simply, throwing a lure from dock or boat proves to be very effective at this time of year. Cast your jig or lure towards shore then count to three after the jig hits the water. Retrieve a short distance, let it sink etc. The fish will usually strike on the fall. Gradually increase your count with each cast until you find the depth where the fish are holding then continue to target that depth. Work in a radius from the point you are casting from; moving on once you have covered all of the accessible water from where you are standing. This method is extremely effective when the fish have moved into the shallows and are tightly grouped. It is a lot of fun when you get into the fish and a great way to get kids interested in fishing. Target the shallow areas off points, shallow protected bays and areas with grass where you can expect to find bug hatches.

Spoons such as the Krocodile by Luhr Jensen, Acme's Kastmaster, and the Tasmanian Devil by Wigston lures in assorted colors work very well. Use a good rod with either a low profile casting reel or a spinning reel and a rod with a medium fast action so you can get some real distance in your casts. When fishing from a boat I like to anchor off the bank far enough so I can get good long casts in a half radius and cover a lot of water while prospecting. Once I find the fish I can adjust my location to better target the hot spots. A real slick setup for this type of fishing is an electric trolling motor with a remote. The remote will allow you to slowly move down the shoreline or maintain a position when you find a hot spot; leaving your hands free to cast, catch and land fish.

The catch before breakfast, I came in and had breakfast then went back out for another banner day on Wickiup Reservoir!

Vertical Jigging:

Vertical jigging is especially effective in the early spring/winter when fish are schooled up and feeding off fresh water shrimp and bug larvae. During this short period of time you can easily catch large numbers of fish fairly quickly. You can locate the fish by one of several methods; trolling, using your fish finder or just heading out to where the boats are in a group. Anchor up both front and rear to keep from swinging around in the wind. Another common method of avoiding the drift is to tie off to the debris boom in front of a dam. Lower your jig to depth with consistent pulls of the line until you reach the fish. A good example of this is that I commonly pull off two feet of line with each pull. Someone with shorter arms will pull off less. You can measure the distance from the reel to the first eye and use that measurement to compute the depth as well. The idea is to develop a good system to accurately target the right depth. If you don't know the correct depth, lower in stages until you find the fish. Once you have the right depth, mark your line with a piece of tape or a bobber stop knot so you can quickly get back in the strike zone after landing a fish. Raising the rod two to three feet and letting it fall, fluttering the rod tip up and down, swimming the jig back and forth will all work. Crippled herring, Buzz Bombs, and colored grubs on a lead head jig are all effective for this type of jigging. The key to good jigging technique is to be one with your line and your rod. Try and sense or feel the bite which can be a subtle as a slight bump or as strong as a normal strike. The better you get at sensing the strike, the more fish you will put in the boat. Don't drop your rod tip so fast you have a lot of slack line, instead keep enough tension on the rod so as the lure falls you can still "feel" the jig. You will notice right off the bat one or two boats will be catching the majority of the fish. It isn't because they are in the right spot, it is because they have mastered the sensitivity required to continually catch fish. Watch those around you that are being successful. Modify your technique to what they are doing in not only bait type and color but also the technique they are using. Be friendly and ask questions because many better anglers are more than willing to share information, you just need to ask!

There is some key equipment required for good results when jigging. I covered part of this in the rod and reel section of chapter 3. The 2nd and probably the most important part is line type. Because of line stretch with monofilament line, there is too much distance and in this case time between lifting the rod for the hook set and the actual hook set due to line stretch. Mono (monofilament) has stretch qualities which are very forgiving in lots of situations but in this case will cut way down on the fish you actually put in your boat. Mono has a stretch of up to 20% depending on the brand and quality of the line. For example, if your line has a rating of 10% stretch and you are fishing in 30' of water, the line will stretch three feet or more before the hook at the end of your line reacts to the raise of the rod. By that time the fish may have moved on. Braided low stretch line is highly recommended for this type of fishing. Tuff Line, Stren, and Spider Wire all produce good braided low stretch lines which work well for this purpose. Tuff Line has recently come out with a color coded line called Indicator. The color changes every ten feet so by counting the colors you can quickly get down to depth eliminating the sometimes confusing use of pulls. Because braided line is naturally limp, it will sometimes have the tendency to pass the jig and get tangled in the hook(s). To avoid this happening, just tie on thirty inches of stiff leader between the braid and the jig. Because you are only raising your jig a foot or so, the braid will never come in contact with the hook or hooks if you do this.

Jig color also plays a big part in the process. Make sure you have a selection of colors in the major color group. Green, pink, orange, blue, purple, silver and gold all will play a role at one time or another. UV and Glow products are extremely effective at drawing the strike with Glow being the better of the two. Kokanee's moods change on a whim so when the bite changes so must you by offering something different in the way of color or scent.

Scents for jigging are another way of providing an added incentive to bite. By adding a scent or scented gel to your offering, you are definitely increasing the attraction of your offering. Picture the jig moving up and down with a small portion of scent or scented gel applied to the jig body. As the lure moves, scent is washed off the lure body creating a scent cloud around the jig which will and does incite more fish to move towards the lure or general location. Kind of reminds me of a fresh tray of cookies coming out of the oven, you just can't pass it up without investigating. The new gel scents from Pro-Cure last a long time when applied to a lure body and have the advantage of also having a UV enhancer which will draw more focus to your moving jig. For scents, I would first recommend crayfish and shrimp because small crustaceans make up a big part of the Kokanee diet in spring. You can and should experiment with the rest of the scents but I would just start with those two and work up.

Bait while jigging is used by many and scorned by many others. If you feel it gives you an edge, use it. If you don't, well you get the picture. I don't, but I do use scent. The decision is yours.

Still Bait Fishing:

Still bait fishing adds another complete dimension to pursuing Kokanee. The key to this type of fishing is to station your boat over a tight school of Kokanee, and anchor up front and rear. The anchor falling might spook the fish away but if you are patient, they will move back in to the general area. I like to use a short stiff leader attached to the braided low stretch line of my jigging rod. My goal is to position the bait right over the school or in the midst of it. I then sit patiently without moving the rod. A strike is indicated by a bobble or dip of the rod tip at which time I set the hook and hopefully bring in a silver Kokanee for the box. I have had the best luck with this system in the spring just before the Kokanee start to head out on the lake to feed on zooplankton. That brief window can be as long as a week and as short as a day or two. If you are lucky to hit this window, you will have stumbled onto the mother lode. I position a couple of spit shot on my line six inches above the bait to keep my bait stationary and to help get the bait to depth quickly. A jig body with thirty inches of stiff leader above and a short six inch piece below works quite well in place of the split shot when there is much depth involved. The upper leader keeps you from getting tangles and the lower leader separates the jig head from the bait. My best results have come from a small treble hook with the hooks bent out slightly.

For bait, I will use small pieces of crayfish tails, Pautzke's Balls of Fire, Powerbait grubs, Powerbait® sparkle dough, or scented and dyed corn. One piece on each tine of the hook will suffice although I am sure just one piece on one of the tines would work.

The use of scent is almost mandatory when using this technique because the scent will spread out around your bait and hook; hopefully driving the fish into attack mode.

Trolling:

Trolling is by far my favorite method of targeting Kokanee and can be effectively used year around. During the spring, just as with jigging, you target the shallows. The beauty of trolling is that you can cover lots of water during the course of the day and in the process locating the largest populations of fish. There are two types of spring trolling covered here: long lining and downrigger fishing. Both of these methods are effective and both have their pros and con's.

Long lining is by far my favorite when trolling in the spring. In long lining there are no weights or downriggers involved. The standard equipment is just an eight pound mono line, a dodger and a lure, spinner, or hoochie of choice. For all trolling applications covered here, monofilament line is the standard. I won't be covering lead, copper, steel line or the use of lead weights. If you are interested in these techniques I would suggest you try one of several good trolling books which are available. My focus here is to expose the reader to the use of lighter tackle where the fight of the fish can be experienced firsthand through the action of the rod. There is nothing wrong with those techniques; they are just not my favorite form of targeting Kokanee.

Trolling Speed:

Trolling speed has been a contentious issue for several years now. Many of the old timers swear by the .9 Mph to 1.2 Mph rule. I don't feel there is any hard and fast rule concerning speed. I use the speed which catches fish. In the spring, lure and dodger type are the main factors which regulate my speed. Run your lure and dodger of choice over the side of the boat where you can easily observe them and vary the forward speed up or down until you find the optimum speed. Too fast and the dodger will roll. Too slow and there will be no action. Experiment and don't be afraid to try something new! Different dodgers work better at faster speeds such as the offerings from Shasta Tackle and Father Murphy and vise versa. The faster you troll, the less bend you want in your dodger.

Long Lining:

As the name implies, you are fishing with a lot of line off the rear of the boat. Because of this, care must be taken while making turns with the boat. This technique does not require a lot of equipment other than a good boat and a trolling motor that will hold the speed down between .5 Mph and 1.8 Mph. It is helpful to have a depth finder so you can avoid losing tackle on submerged logs, stumps and ridges. Line counter reels are nice when using this technique but not absolutely necessary. Once you achieve the optimum line out distance put a piece of tape or a bobber stop on the line so the next time you run your line out you can do so quickly. Since you are targeting fish in the spring, they will typically be found in the shallower areas of the lake where the sunshine has had the ability to raise the temperature of the water and in the process stimulate the hatch of fresh water shrimp, mayflies, damsel flies and Chironomids Etc. In addition to Kokanee many other species of fish will be found in the shallows during this time period. Because of this, don't be surprised if you catch fish such as German browns and Lake trout.

Mack's Lures Double "D" dodger. This is a cool dodger because it is directional, controlled by the four hookup points in the front of the dodger. This dodger works well at higher speeds as well as the slower speeds providing a forward and backward motion unlike other dodgers.

I usually start by letting out between ninety and one hundred feet of line once I am underway. I do this by using equal pulls of line off my reel. A pull of line is different for everyone so it is a good idea to get to know how far it is from the front of the reel to the first eye on your trolling rod. That way you can make a judgment call as to how long your pulls really are and in the process know just how many pulls get you one hundred feet behind the boat. If you are running more than two rods, you will probably want to use inline side planers. You would do this in much the same fashion as mentioned above except once you get your line out the distance you decided upon you would hook in a side planer set up for the side of the boat that you will be running it off of. At that point, let out enough line to get a good spread from the side of the boat so you are not crossing lines in a long turn. Once both sides are out, you then let out the lines which will come off on either side of the stern. Side planers are available from both Sep's Pro fishing and Yellow Bird which will work well for this situation. The Yellow Bird versions come with a strike indicator which is a nice feature. The Sep's Pro Tackle version is reversible so it can be used on either side of the boat by just reversing the arm. You can also run more than one side planer off either side of the boat giving you the ability to fish more rods at once. Just be aware, the more complicated you make it the worse the snarls when something goes wrong. One of the things I like about side planer fishing in the spring is that it allows you to fish your outside rods much shallower. By shortening the setback from the planer to the dodger on the end of your line, you can reduce the depth which will allow you to run a lure in fairly shallow water which would otherwise be hard to target when trolling, making side planers a real cool accessory! Not only are you able to fish the shallow edge of the lake, you have no boat shadow spooking the fish which will give you more opportunity to target fish which otherwise would be spooked by the shadow of the boat.

One of the tricks of running a long line out the rear is to be able to get a line quickly back to the same spot after a fish is landed. By paying attention to the distance the line plays out behind the boat before hitting the water, you can easily estimate the correct distance without using a line counter reel or even pulls of line. When paying out line, keep the rod at the same angle and rod tip height and play out the line by keeping your thumb on the spool. When it looks like you are close, apply pressure to the spool stopping the line from paying out and compare the line to one of the others and adjusting till they match.

Never stop your forward motion when trolling in shallow water if you have several lines out. If you do, you are probably going to be spending a lot of time untangling and not enough time fishing. It is a bummer that with spring fishing, you are going to be losing tackle to sunken logs and debris. Plan for it and move on, but don't stop when you have a chance of losing much more than one lure.

Father Murphy: Mini Dodgers

The dodger size when long lining will make a big difference when you are trolling in shallow water. Heavier dodgers such as Vance's Tackle dodgers will actually pull your line down deeper, especially when fishing slowly. Bump up the speed slightly, or shorten the setback if you are tapping bottom to pick your presentation up a bit or even change out to a lighter dodger such as the smaller Shasta Sling Blade. As spring progresses and the fish are found deeper, the heavier dodger will pay off by taking your presentation down to them.

Another good use of long lining is in conjunction with downriggers so you are not stacking lines. I will run my downrigger lines shorter, say with a fifty foot setback and my long lines at ninety or a hundred. That keeps all of my lines in 'shallow' mode for targeting the spring bite.

Downrigger Trolling:

Downrigger trolling in the spring is fairly simple in that you don't have near the cable down as you will later in the summer as the water warms up. Pay particular attention to the water depth so you don't get your weights hung up on submerged objects. This is the time of year when manual downriggers are not such a pain! When using downriggers in the spring, I like to run a setback between twenty and fifty feet depending on the depth. The deeper we are running, the

shorter the setback. Because you are running shallow, and have so much line out, stacking is not an option as it will be later in the year. I like to run one line on either side of the boat right off the downrigger weight. Because you are running shallow, the weights can be fairly light, even in the four pound range since there is little line drag from water resistance. Since you are running one line on each downrigger, you can either run additional long lines off the rear of the boat or with in-line side planer boards. The downrigger gives you more accurate depth control especially when fishing in

Crystal Basin Wild Thing Mini Dodgers

areas where the depth changes constantly.

Dodgers:

Dodgers that seem to work best in the spring, at least for me, are the nickel blades as opposed to the painted with the exception of black. Black will work well on those overcast days when nothing else works. Copper and gold also work very well. In that case, I also like smaller dodgers such as the 4/0 or one of the mini dodgers such as Crystal Basin's Wild Thing or Sep's Side Kick, both of which are very small by dodger standards. Another trick is to use Wobblers with the hook removed and replaced with a good snap swivel. Wobblers can be found in the salmon lure section of your local sporting goods supply and come in a variety of colors and finishes. They work very well when trolling slowly, giving off good flash and a reduced thump or sound. A unique dodger which works well long lining is the Mack's Double D dodger which can be set to avoid lines getting crossed when running multiple lines. Just clip into the appropriate indexing hole on the front of the dodger and it will pull your line out to one side or the other depending on the setting you choose.

Flashers or gang trolls:

Flashers or gang trolls can be very effective when Kokanee are schooled up tight in the spring. I am not a big fan of gang trolls because the less gear you have in line with your lure the better the fight. However, results can speak volumes when the action is slow and many times, I would have returned home with nothing in the box if it hadn't been for the use of this fish attractor. There are a plethora of products out there which fit this category but only a few I prefer to use. The age old Cowbell and Beer Can trolls are still seen on a regular basis. Because of my aversion to lots of heavy in-line gear, I gravitate towards the light weight lake trolls now available. Some of the higher quality lake trolls are made by Vance's, Sep's Pro Fishing and

Mack's Lure. Vance's are at the outside extreme of my favorites in that they are the heaviest. The middle of the road would be Sep's, still very high quality but a bit heavy. The lightest of the group are Mack's which are made with Mylar and are truly light weight, almost to the point you can't even feel they are there. Each of these has a place in the serious Kokanee angler's tackle box and all of them work well in the right place and time. Vance's lake trolls are a little heavier and I prefer them when long lining in slightly deeper water. If there is one thing I hate it is losing tackle to the bottom or to sunken logs or stumps. If this is an issue, I will go with the next heaviest of the three when long lining,

A nice Kokanee caught using an R&K hoochie and a Shasta Sling Blade.
Photo courtesy of Jeremy Jahn

which is the Sep's Pro Flasher system. With a lighter weight, I seem to get hung up less while still having good success in attracting fish.

The lightest of the flasher systems I use are the Flash Lite trolls made by Mack's. I like to run these on my downriggers because they are light and have very little drag. Because there is so little drag, they don't cause the downrigger clips to release prematurely while at the same time giving off a very effective flash and attracting fish.

When buying lake trolls, some things to look for are: blade quality, cable instead of rigid

Shasta Tackle: Troll Lite

stainless wire and quality swivels and snaps. Lake trolls are not cheap, so when you buy, look for quality!

Since lake trolls will not impart action to lures, it is important to select lures which have action of their own. Spoons, Spinners and Plugs are all good selections for running behind a lake troll. Depending on the lake you are fishing, leader lengths of twenty four inches and up work well. One lake which comes to mind is Paulina Lake. Leader lengths upward of six feet long are the rule there rather than the exception.

Spinners:

Fishing with spinners in the spring has always been one of my favorite techniques. Crystal Basin, Father Murphy, Mack's Lure, R&K and Shasta Tackle all put out good quality spinners which will work right out of the package.

My first experience with spinners was years ago as a kid fishing with Wedding Ring Spinners by Mack's Lure. They were at one time the "must have" bait at most lakes here in Oregon and I

am sure most other places. They are still hot at most lakes and with the new versions which incidentally have the Smile Blade technology you have even more variety. The things I look for most in a good spinner is finish quality, both Glow and UV as well as quality hooks. If spinners purchased over the counter don't have good hooks, definitely replace them with high quality laser hooks in either drop shot or octopus hook by Gamakatsu or another high quality hook such as the Sickle hook by Matsuo. A word to the wise, laser sharpened hooks should be

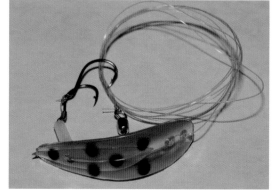
Apex in Water Mellon by Hot-Spot

replaced not sharpened in my opinion. The cost of the hook verses the loss of fish due to a poor sharpening job just doesn't add up enough to justify not replacing them. I originally started fishing the spinners with the entire leader which came with them, sometimes upwards of five or six feet. Today, my average leader length on my spinners is only twelve to twenty four inches. There are a few lakes where longer leaders work better, but they are more the exception than the rule.

Spoons:

Another great attractor comes in the form of spoons. Spoons are probably one of the most underutilized baits for Kokanee here in the northwest. I am sure they are a little more popular down in Northern California than up here in Oregon and Washington, but regardless of that, they are responsible for many fish which end up in my fish box. Companies like Apex, Dick Nite, Luhr Jensen, Sep's, and Vance's Tackle all produce great smaller spoons which work well for targeting Kokanee in the spring. Once again, the Glow and UV colors are my favorites and the most productive. Buy these in the major color groups; green, pink, orange, red, blue, purple and black. That's right, black is a very effective color for lures of any type in overcast conditions. Salmon fishermen here in the northwest have known this for years, and it is about time Kokanee fishermen started using this to their advantage as well. The leader should be between eighteen and thirty inches behind the dodger to allow the most natural action of the spoon. On some of the smaller spoons like Vance's Sockeye Slammer, take a pair of needle nose pliers and slightly bend the hook out. That simple trick will help to cut down on short bites.

Another great trick which has been around for many years is to add a second hook to the spoon of choice. Take a small piece of surgical tubing or cut a piece out of a Kokanee bungee and slide it over the end of a light hook. Then stick the point of the hook attached to the lure through the surgical tubing and the eye of the hook. Make sure the second hook is facing in the opposite direction as the first hook for best results. This will help to catch the fish that is short biting and will also help to eliminate fish which are rolling up in the line to throw the hook.

One final spoon trick is to change out the hook with a high quality wire hook. The heavier Siwash hooks just don't perform as well as the lighter wire hooks of choice. Once again I prefer the high quality laser hooks in drop shot, Sickle or octopus by Gamakatsu or Matsuo.

Hoochies or Squids:

Hoochies as I know them are some of the most effective baits available on the market today. They are simple yet very effective no matter what time of the year you are using them. Straight hoochies have no action of their own and as such need to be run tight to a dodger to give them enough action to entice a bite. When I first started using them, I didn't have a whole lot of confidence in them and they didn't get as much time in the game as some of my players which had proven themselves. Once I learned the trick of

Three Micro hoochies produced by R&K Spinners

shortening the leader, they were back in the game! I like to run hoochies with a leader length of between eight and twelve inches. You can run one effectively up to sixteen inches but I have found over years of testing the shorter lengths as stated above are the more consistent producers.

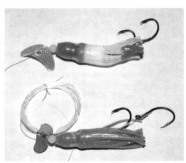

Mack's Lure: Cha Cha

When looking for hoochies, buy the Glow and UV version in all of the basic colors, especially the ones with sparkles added. All of the major tackle companies have their own versions and color shades. Some of the producers to look for are: Crystal Basin, Mack's Tackle, Sep's Pro Fishing, Shasta Tackle, R&K Spinners, and Vance's Tackle. Any good Kokanee hoochie or squid should have a double hook set up. I prefer the bottom of the upper hook to be even with the eye of the lower hook. If I get a pre-tied hoochie and the hook system does not meet my personal standards, I will re-tie it with my hooks of choice and with the spacing I prefer.

One of my reasons for the spacing of the hook and also the quality of the hooks is that many times a fish will take the rear hook and roll up in the line. When they do that, the second hook will usually end up in the gill plate and ensuring the fish will be landed. If you are out fishing one day and lose a fish for some reason, notice the skirt of the hoochie is almost always pushed up the line. That is why I prefer high quality laser cut sticky sharp hooks. The fish probably rolled up your line until it had enough leverage and in the process ripped or loosened the lower hook. With sticky sharp hooks this problem is greatly reduced. I also like to tie my own hoochies; in fact I make many of my mini squid setups. You can buy your hoochie or squid bodies in bulk and produce your own.

Plugs:

There are a few smaller plugs which seem to work well when trolling in the spring, especially when long lining. One longtime favorite in the Northwest is the flat fish which has gained great popularity with trout and salmon fishermen. The smaller versions of these plugs work very well when used on the spring Kokanee fishery. Wee Tad's or Wee Thing which is produced by Crystal Basin can work well when trolled behind the downrigger. For fishing these plug type baits with action of their own, use longer leaders behind the dodger so the seductive action of the plug is not inhibited by the action of the dodger.

Alternate Baits:

When fishing in the spring, I have had real good luck with plastic baits intended for Walleye, bass or crappie fishing. Curly tailed grubs, crappie tubes, pink worms, and multicolored minnows all work very well. What I usually do while at a sporting goods store is look at all of the bulk packages of baits. I select a good variety of color, scent and shape or style.

An assortment of tried and proven alternate baits. PowerBait dough bait works well for jigging and bait fishing

All of the scented baits like Yum, Berkley and several others which are usually located in the same area work very well.

The trick to using these baits is to have some pre-tied double hook sets set aside specifically for this purpose. Many of the scented versions are good for one day only since once the hooks are applied, it is hard to keep them fresh. I carry a needle in one of my boxes specifically for setting up these baits. Just take one of the pre-tied leaders and thread the leading loose end an inch or so through the needle and then insert the needle through the trailing end of the bait and out the front. Tie a loop in the loose end of the leader and you are in business. Since these baits have little action of their own, I usually use the same set back as I would when running hoochies. Curly tailed grubs do have some action and can be run with a slightly longer leader. You can either store your leaders in a leader caddy or on a piece of pipe insulation tube purchased at a home improvement center. These can be purchased for as little as a dollar for a six foot section which can be cut to a convenient storage size.

Streamer flies also work well when targeting Spring Kokanee. Once again, pick out flies that cover the major color groups and use them in much the same fashion as you would hoochies or any other bait with no action of its own. There are also some commercially produced bugs on the market specially designed for Kokanee. These should be run in much the same fashion as previously mentioned.

As you can see from the methods outlined in this chapter, there are many different ways to put fish in the boat. Many never learn to do more than one method which is a shame; kind of like eating the same peanut butter sandwich for three meals seven days a week. I enjoy using multiple methods of fishing during the course of the year. It also gives you the advantage of moving on to a different approach on the days your favorite method isn't working. It is kind of funny that there are guys and gals who are either jiggers or trollers seldom straying to the other methods available.

There is also the issue of tackle which can be rather limiting due to the cost involved. Rather than going out and spending a small fortune to get all of the tackle to attack all of the methods covered here, buy a little at a time, and work your way up. By approaching it this way it will not be nearly as painful when you inevitably lose some of your gear to the tackle racks lining the bottom of the lakes. Remember, fishing is supposed to be fun so in order to keep it so, don't bring the stress of finances into the peaceful days out on the lake.

Metolius Arm of Lake Billy Chinook

5 ...Summer and Early Fall

One year I was camped on Wickiup Reservoir in Central Oregon and struck up a conversation with the fellow camped next door. He was an avid Chinook angler living in the Portland area and had access to the Columbia and the Willamette rivers literally in his back yard. He had gone fishing with some friends on the Deschutes channel that week and caught a few Kokanee jigging and trolling with salmon and steelhead rods. He was not impressed and after his friends had departed for home; had no interest in pursuing Kokanee any further. Every day I would come in with my catch. He would admire the size and quantity of fish, relating how after fishing all day they had only caught a few. One evening I asked him if he would like to go out with me the next day and give it a try. The next morning we got into the fish right away, boating fish after fish with three or four doubles in the process while using downriggers and light weight trolling rods. Needless to say, he had a great time of constant action. His comment was that my fishing style was more like science than fishing as he knew it. I like that description, "fishing science" pretty much says it all!

Once the zooplankton gets established, the Kokanee populations will spread out over the lake

*A beautiful summer day on **Wickiup Reservoir in Central Oregon***

and feed much like cattle. I really fight the temptation to call them herds, but if you have ever looked out on the open fields of the West, and seen the herds grazing on fields of fresh grass, you have an idea how Kokanee behave. The thermo cline comes into play more and more as the summer progresses. The warmer surface temperatures start rising until they feel like bath water radically dropping the waters ability to hold the oxygen required for both the fish and for the zooplankton. As the water temperatures rise, the thermo cline is pushed deeper in the lake.

If you were to idle across the lake with no lines or downriggers in the water, and the sensitivity turned up on your fish finder, chances are, you will notice a distinct layer or line where the warmer water meets the cooler more stable water. It is this line which will determine your ultimate success at consistently catching Kokanee. Find this line, keep your presentation within ten to fifteen feet on either side of it and you will eventually find the fish whether you can see them on the fish finder or not.

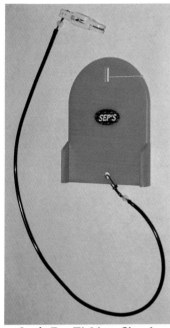

Sep's Pro Fishing: Simply Trolling Device

Another way to locate this line is by lowering a thermometer either on a downrigger, a hand line or a fishing rod. The Vexilar thermometer mentioned in chapter 2 is specifically made for this purpose and can cut way down on your prospecting time. If you are fishing in too warm of water, chances are you will spend a lot of time catching nothing but if you locate the thermo cline, you will have found the key ingredient to finding fish or at least Kokanee.

In many lakes, the fish will have a fairly set pattern as to where they are located at any given part of the year. You can find this information by talking to people at lodges or stores located on the lake or by talking to other fishermen. By being friendly, you can usually find someone who is willing to part with enough information to get you into the fish.

This time of year, trolling is usually the method of choice for consistently catching fish. Early in the season, open up an occasional fish and look at the contents of its digestive tract. Once the contents become mostly zooplankton, the spring season is officially over and you can expect the fish to follow the thermo cline and move out over the lake. Once this happens the most productive method is going to be trolling with downriggers.

Downrigger fishing in the summer season is much different than in the spring. For starters, you can fish much closer to the ball with your dodger and lure of choice. I prefer to be no further from the ball, in most cases, than twelve feet. The fish will become much more aggressive as the summer season moves along and the adult fish become mature and start closing in on the spawning season. As in the spring, flash will attract more fish, but in this case we are given the option of losing the gang trolls and replacing them with ball trolls. Ball trolls are a longer set of gang trolls designed to be clipped to the downrigger balls or to the downrigger cable. The downrigger release is clipped onto the downrigger cable three to five feet above the ball or ball troll. Some like to put the release clip at the end

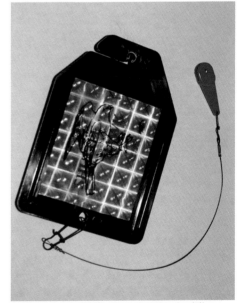

Shasta Tackle's Shuttle Hawk. These devices take the work out of manual downriggers by quickly carrying your line back down to depth. Tip: Run a heavy rubber band from front to rear of the Shuttle Hawk to keep it from slipping off the downrigger cable.

of the ball troll, however, the disadvantage of clipping the release right onto the ball troll is that any resistance on the line pulls the tail end of the troll up stopping the action of the blades. Because of this, I like to hook on three to five feet above the ball troll. Ball trolls are produced by several quality tackle makers some of which are: Vance's Tackle, Sep's Pro fishing, Shasta Tackle, and Crystal Basin. I like to run my dodger just a couple of feet past the end of the ball troll. By running the lines this short, I am able to make tight turns when a "herd" of fish is located and make several passes through the school without making the wide sweeping turns required with long setbacks from the ball. This gives me the advantage of targeting the school before it moves. Many times we will have two or more fish on at one time and as we land the last fish, I will hit the man overboard button on the remote which will make the autopilot turn and take us right back over the same spot. While the boat is making the turns, the fishermen and women are free to re bait and get their lines back down to depth without worrying about steering the boat!

When fishing with downriggers during the summer and early fall, I prefer to stack my rods. Stacking is the simple procedure of using a stacking release and spacing lines out down the downrigger cable five to ten feet apart. With the two rod stamp available now in many Western states, this enables you to get multiple baits in the water at varied depths and cover more of the water column. By varying the depth from one side of the boat to the other, you can have bait or lure every four or five feet in the water column near the thermo cline which allows you to prospect more water in less time. Once you find a hot bait color, type or depth, you can move other rods in your spread over to the hot color/bait and when the bite cools, move back to multiple colors and types of bait.

Trolling Speed:

Trolling speed has been an area of contention now for several years. With the advent of GPS, tracking your speed has become very simple and fairly accurate. If you don't have GPS, a simple device made and sold by Luhr Jensen will help you to facilitate an accurate speed. For me, the best trolling speed has always been the one that is catching fish! Sometimes trolling fast will put fish in the boat and sometimes trolling slow will put fish in the boat. There is no hard and fast rule when determining this except that it will vary from lake to lake and day to day. My advice is to be flexible and willing to change. If you always do what you have always done, chances are you will always get what you have always had. Be spontaneous and try new speeds! The old standard was .9 Mph to 1.2 Mph. That speed has worked well for me in the past and I am sure it will work well in the future. I have also had very good luck from .5 Mph clear up to 2.1 Mph and that is the fastest I have intentionally trolled for Kokanee. That doesn't mean I can't catch fish going faster, it just means I haven't tried it yet! In saying that, I probably won't be going 2.1 Mph on a regular basis unless I continue to have luck going that fast. I will however, troll at speeds from .5 Mph all the way up to 2.1, if it means catching fish. Rules of this sort are made to be broken and cannot be applied to every situation. If you are trolling along at 1.2 Mph and not getting any action, try making some hard left and right hand turns which will load up the outside rod and take the load off the inside rod. If that changes your luck, and you get bit on one side or the other, either increase or decrease you speed to emulate that. The rule of thumb while making turns is that the outside rod speeds up and the inside rod slows down. Once you determine which rod is getting the bite, adjust your speed up or down to match the rod getting hit.

Kokanee hooked and landed with a pink hoochie with a small bead and a Spin-N-Glow with one wing clipped off to make the hoochie wobble

Gang Trolls or Lake Trolls:

As previously stated in the prior chapter, I am not a big fan of gang or lake trolls, but

Assorted Flashers from Left: Vance's Tackle and Sep's Pro Fishing

sometimes they are the most effective method of putting fish in the boat. As the summer progresses, the more effective these become. I will usually run these fairly tight to the ball with no more than a five or six foot setback to the start of the gang troll. When stacking I will run the gang troll on the bottom.

I like to run the upper rod with just a dodger and space it out similar to the method used for running a ball troll with my dodger and bait or lure trailing slightly behind the end of the gang troll. The troll will bring the fish in and the lure following the dodger will bring in the fish which miss the lure following the gang troll. When stacking in this situation, be sure to drop your weights slowly enough so the lower line does not get tangled with the upper line. I have also found when stacking, under most circumstances, it is better to have the releases set to where they release upon the strike. If the release is set too stiff, the fish will, in its quest for freedom, get tangled up with the other stacked line. If the fish is released from the clip upon the strike, it will drift back clear of the other stacked line most of the time.

If when using lake trolls, you are experiencing a lot of releases prior to getting the fish to the boat, try using trolling snubbers behind the lake troll. These will act as a shock absorber to the system. The problem with the lake trolls is that they inhibit the shock absorbing qualities of the monofilament and the light trolling rod. With the addition of this inexpensive item you can eliminate many of the spin offs caused by this.

Dodgers:

A selection of Sep's Pro Fishing's dodgers should be in any serious Kokaholic's tackle box

Dodgers have now been covered a couple of times so far. How much difference can there be from one season to the next you might ask? The truth is a dodger will work basically the same whether it is spring, summer or fall. Many times when the bite is hot, I won't even run a dodger, just a spinner or lure. The less drag, the better the fight! As the season matures and fall is nearing, mature Kokanee will get much more aggressive. You will notice slight changes, such as the slight hooking of the jaw. Once you start seeing this occur, try using larger dodgers or dodgers with more flash. My choice for more flash would be large nickel or preferably gold dodgers. Gold puts off an incredible amount of flash and has some very good attention getting qualities. The only down side to this is in lakes where there is heavy predation by other fish such as Lake trout. In which case, use dodgers with as little bend as possible or even go-to lake trolls. Picture the hard pump of from the tail of a large predatory fish; that movement creates vibration and vibration is a fish's first line of defense. Less vibration is best in this type of situation and sometimes subdued flash as well. Dodgers such as those produced by Shasta Tackle, Father Murphy and Rocky Mountain Tackle work well; when too much thump or faster trolling speed is an issue. There is only one reduced bend on Shasta's large Sling Blade dodger which means less vibration or thump; but you can still get the flash if that is what you want. Dodgers like this work well in lakes such as Northeastern Oregon's Wallowa Lake where the fish compete with large and aggressive Mackinaw. Because you will be fishing at greater depth, painted dodgers should be Glow and UV enhanced. While fishing in the latter part of summer it is not uncommon to be fishing at 65 feet or more depending on the time of day and the lake you are fishing at. Glow dodgers like those sold by Sep's Pro

A good assortment of Vance's Tackle dodgers

Fishing work well in this situation. Referring back to the color spectrum found in chapter 1, choose colors which are readily seen at greater depths if you are not using glow or fluorescent colors. Purple and violet are some of my favorite colors, especially when the lack of light penetration compounded by heavy plankton bloom is brought into the picture.

LIGHTBULB MOMENT ☼ one trick to reduce the thump of normal dodgers such as Vance's and Sep's is to apply split shot to the leader just downstream from the dodger. By adding a few split shot you can adjust a standard dodger to fit almost any trolling situation. Use the type of split shot that have the small ears on them for easy removal. Run your dodger over the side of the boat and test it at the trolling speed of choice to see how much you have actually reduced the movement of the dodger.

Another cool product which works well when fishing deep and stacking lines on a downrigger is the Mack's Double D dodger. This dodger is a directional dodger which can be adjusted to run off to one side or the other depending on the side of the boat it is on. You can set the bottom dodger to go one way and the upper stacked dodger to go the other. By doing this you greatly reduce the chances of getting the upper and lower lines tangled. When the line releases, the dodger is already off to one side or the other and just drifts back until the slack is out of the line.

LIGHTBULB MOMENT ☼ another very effective trick is to add holographic tape and shattered eyes to a dodger. You can either apply one color or multiple colors to the dodger. I like do this on dodgers where the finish or paint has started to come off. The shattered eyes seem to add a whole new dimension to the attraction values of the dodger. You can purchase shattered eyes by the card at many good sportsman's supplies.

Spoons:

Most lures that are effective in the spring are still effective during the summer with a few caveats. Glow and UV become even more important the deeper you fish. Because of the depth, light penetration is much less than when fishing in the first thirty feet of water as in the spring. Compound this with the full bloom of plankton common at this time of year and you have radically reduced the amount of light available. UV rays are the first to disappear as the depth progresses although in my opinion having UV is better than no enhancement at all.

Glow products were not as common a few years ago as they are now. When I started using UV enhanced products I had a very noticeable increase in strikes which resulted in more fish in the box. With the addition of glow products, that increase in catch has compounded much like I would like to see in my retirement account (wishful thinking). Most of the producers of quality tackle now have glow products on the market. This facet of the Kokanee fishery is one of the latest to unfold. Every year, I see improvements in the glow products available. Some

Spoons: Top 3-Vance's Tackle Sockeye Slammers, Bottom; 2-Shasta Tackle Hum Dingers

of the better products will glow for up to six hours or more. One thing I would encourage the Kokanee fanatic to do is to pay attention to the products that are available whether intended for Kokanee or not. If it looks like it is the right size and will catch Kokanee, it probably will. I have had more and more success with things which looked good especially now glow products are available. Apex, Crystal Basin, Dick Nite, Mack's, Pro-Troll, Sep's, Shasta, and many more produce spoons with glow and fluorescent features. I am sure my wife cringes every time I enter a sporting goods store because I seldom walk out without something to add to my collection. One of the standing jokes with Kokanee fishermen (commonly called kokaholics) is that the only thing more expensive than a Kokanee fisherman's boat is his tackle box or boxes as in my case. I have boxes and boxes of lures, spoons, spinners and plugs. I have bags of bulk hoochies, grubs, worms, crank baits etc…

Plugs:

Plugs are extremely effective when fished deep for larger Kokanee. I like to run a plug on the bottom of a stacked set. Larger fish seem to hang just below the school (or herd). The slow wobble back and forth offered by a smaller plug is a good addition to any array you might be running. Wee Tads and plugs like them, where the plug actually will slide up the line away from the fish and in the process avoiding the hook pulling leverage a traditional plug offers; are go-to large Kokanee producing lures. I will usually fish at least one plug four or five feet below the rest of my offerings in search of the larger fish that is usually hanging below the rest of the school. Many of these larger fish will also be found alone, away from the school. Pay particular attention to the fish finder and you will see what I am talking about!

ProTroll: Trout Killer with E Chip Technology

Because of the depth you are operating at when trolling with downriggers during the latter part of the summer season, it is simply a good practice to keep a close eye on your rod and lines. When a fish pulls free of the downrigger clip or worse yet, when they don't, you will need to quickly take the slack out of the line. Slack line has always been a problem no matter what type of fish you are pursuing with maybe an exception of catfish which inevitably swallow the hook. For this reason a good quality reel with a high retrieve ratio is the key to landing more fish. Once the slack is out of the line, you can take your time playing the fish and let the drag and the flex of the rod absorb much of the fight so as not to erode the jaw at the end of the line. When playing larger fish, once the slack is out of the line, I prefer to use my thumb as opposed to the drag. I will keep my drag set very light and play the fish by pumping the rod to gain. When the fish decides to run, I will let it go until it has exhausted itself and will quite literally lay on its side to be netted. The key is to keep constant control of your line, not horsing in the fish. Let the fish tire its self out of its own volition while carefully avoiding undue leverage on its jaw. Once you have done this, it is easy to bring the fish in and land it. The secret in all of this is to treat the fish as though it is poorly hooked every time you have a large fish on. You never know how solidly hooked a fish is until it is in the boat. Half the time when they are laying on the floor of the boat the hook will just drop out, having only been held on by a thread and the light tension carefully kept on the line. As the season progresses, the fish will start moving towards the creeks and spawning beds from which they originated. You will notice the schools will become tighter and more concentrated in the cooler waters near those spawning areas. In the case of planted fish in lakes which have no suitable spawning areas the fish will still school up tight. They will congregate either in areas of inflow or areas of outflow such as creeks flowing into or out of the lake. Large groups of these fish will pool at the faces of dams and reservoirs. Fish will still display spawning behavior even when there is no place for them to spawn. Trolling through these concentrations of fish can be very productive as can jigging.

Once the fish have attained their full size, they will not continue to put on weight but will instead start conserving energy for the trip up to the spawning beds. During this time of year the fish are highly aggressive, possibly in preparation for protecting the nests once they arrive at their final destination. Large dodgers and larger spoons will work very well when this final phase starts coming into play. Hooked jaws will become more prevalent and some of the fish will start losing scales. Younger fish, which are not ready to spawn in the current season, will be mixed in with the mature fish. I speculate this is because they are a naturally schooling fish. It would also stand to reason there are immature fish which will also head up to the spawning grounds much as in the case of ocean run fish. This time of year, the fish will still be good eating, still a month or two away from moving up the creeks. Even though the fish are mature and not really feeding, they are still inclined to strike out at a lure or jig.

Jigging:

Once the fish start locating off of the spawning areas, in the cool deep water ravines, there is no more effective method of catching and landing fish than using a simple jig technique. When jigging, anchor or drift over the top of the fish, dropping your lure into or just above the school.

Because the territorial nature of the fish is highly enhanced at pre-spawn, jigging can be highly profitable. Use the same method of vertical jigging as in the spring, the only difference being the depth the fish are holding to stay in the cooler water. Use heavier jigs, to not only get your line down to depth but also to keep in touch with your jig which is now in 65 feet of water or more.

Use an assortment of the primary colors, preferably in glow. Raising and allowing the jig to drop while staying in tune to its behavior is the rule of thumb. There is only a split second to set the hook from the time of the strike. No stretch lines are the rule of thumb, not the exception. Remember that if the line stretches 20% at sixty five feet, the line will stretch thirteen feet before you get an adequate hook set. Save yourself a lot of grief and invest in some good quality braid! Tuff Line now has some line out which changes color every ten feet making it easy to gauge quickly how deep your jig really is. Once you have determined the effective depth, put a piece of tape or a bobber stop knot on your line to mark the spot, making it that much faster to get back into the strike zone.

Scents and baits can still help bring on the bite. Even though the fish have started to lose the need to feed, the instinct is still there. It is kind of like the joke where the older gentleman says to the younger kid that even though there is snow on the roof, there is still fire in the furnace. Instinct or mental programming may play into this. I prefer the gels produced by ProCure for this purpose. The gel will hold on a jig virtually all day, while producing a cloud of scent which will drift with the current attracting fish back to your presentation.

No matter which method you choose to use during the summer period, this is by far the most family friendly time of year to be out on the water! My wife will sit and read a book while waiting on the bite, but as soon as there is a bump on her line, she is all business. It is extremely addicting to younger fishermen and women because of the action and wild crazy fight of the fish trying to get free of the hook. My grandson had many a good battle with just such a fish during the course of the summer. Getting your kids or grand kids involved in this sport will give them years of enjoyment throughout their lives.

I would highly recommend you not only learn to troll for Kokanee but that you learn to jig for them as well. Vary the presentation until you find the action and continue to learn from the results, because every day is different while seeking this fickle fish.

Downrigger Fishing is very exciting because you get to land larger fish with little or no resistance between you and the fish. Jigging is an intense sport as well, leading to some huge catches in a very short period of time.

6 ...Late Fall and Winter Fishing

My fishing buddy, Rocky finding a little sun on a nice fall morning

I don't know about you, but after a few months of chasing salmon on the coast or over on the Columbia I start getting the urge to just idle along on one of my favorite lakes and just chill. For others, there is no opportunity to chase the fish on coastal streams so after a few months of watching others catching fish on the TV cabin fever starts to set in. That is where this chapter kicks in! Put the top up and the side curtains on, fire up the propane heater, run your lines over the side and enjoy God's creation from the comfort of your boat with little or no competition from the hordes. If I have just described your situation, then I just may see you out there that is after the "spawn" is over!

Once the fish start getting to the point their backs become distorted and the sides are pink or red and the heads are green, it is time to move on to next year's spawners. At this point the fish are literally close to being the living dead and definitely not good eating. They will move in tight to bays and creek mouths ready for the fall weather to give way to rain. Once the rain comes, the fish will move up the creeks, dig their nests and spawn. Their bodies will provide forage for many other creatures as well as returning nutrients to the natal stream.

Once this has taken place, depending on the lake and the temperature of the area, Kokanee can be taken by many of the methods used in both the spring and the fall.

Trolling will continue to be effective until the fall turnover at which point, Kokanee become less active and will be fairly stationary in schools. Once fall turnover takes place, and depending on water temperature, you can actually target the fish much as you would when spring fishing although usually deeper. Jigging and bait fishing becomes king in the Kokanee anglers rulebook and in some areas, where lake surfaces become frozen, Kokanee are targeted through the ice which is something which I personally have not experienced. In others, boats are still the way to access the schools in lakes remaining ice free.

Fishing strategy for the late fall: when the fish start to gather pre-spawn. Why are the fish there? What are they doing? Are they still good eating? How do you get them to bite? How do I know which fish to keep? These are all questions I get asked every year although not by the same people. The following are some ideas that will hopefully help fisherman become more proficient at fishing in the late fall and winter.

An assortment of Father Murphy dodgers

Trolling:

As I stated earlier, once the fish reach full spawning color, they are not going to be much in the way of table fare although still fun to catch. In the interest of protecting the spawning fish, many lakes have the areas where the fish stage prior to heading upstream marked off and fishing is not allowed. There are many who still do go after the spawning fish simply because they are fun to catch. I am not in favor of this and it is my personal opinion that targeting these fish should be off limits. We as fishermen need to be good stewards of the fish we target or one day there will be limited fishing and the glory days will be a thing of the past much as it is with many of the ocean-run salmon populations.

When the fish are just starting to stage and have slightly pink sides and somewhat hooked jaws, the fish are still good eating and worth catching. Many times, next year's fish will be found mingling with the current year's spawners. Trolling through these schools can be very productive and lead to some nice catches. Larger dodgers and more aggressive presentations seem to be more productive for pre-spawn fall fish.

Try speeding up and slowing down, hard turns to the left and then back to the right seem to incite strikes when nothing else works.

LIGHTBULB MOMENT ☼ I have found when fish seem to develop lock jaw this time of year, rarely attacking your presentation, with several passes through a school, try pegging a red bead six to eight inches in front of the lure and with a chunk of tooth pick. This will bring out the nest protecting behavior of the females. The bead simulates an egg with a smaller nest robbing fish in pursuit.

In my personal experience trolling just doesn't work as well in the cold winter as jigging although I will still use this technique. There is something about slowly trolling across a still lake with the rain softly falling while sitting in the comfort of the cabin, with a propane heater glowing in the background. On some of those days, I really couldn't care less if I catch any fish, being more than happy to have the lake to myself and enjoying the snow covered mountains surrounding the lake. I have had some very good days out trolling during the winter, bringing home some pan sized fresh fish for dinner that night. It may not be as productive as jigging during this time of the year but is sure can be relaxing and enjoyable. Once the weather starts cooling and the water of the lake starts to cool, spring techniques become the rule of thumb on many of the more temperate lakes while in the more frigid areas, fishing deep is the best bet. Not being a spring chicken myself, I prefer the more temperate areas. I like long lining during this time of year simply because it cuts down on things to manage like downriggers and such. When fishing with two or more in the boat, I like using side planers to spread out my lines and cover more water. One of the key advantages to side planers is that when fish are running shallow, they are not distracted by the shadow of the boat passing overhead. By running side planers, I can more effectively fish four people out of my boat without the headache of getting lines crossed and tangled.

Jigging:

During the winter months, jigging can be a great way to get the family out on the water! Nothing like a boat full of people all catching fish and ribbing each other over who is catching the biggest and the most fish. Insulated coveralls and wool caps become the dress of the day along with a thermos of hot coffee and maybe a little brandy or Kahlua along with sandwiches and snacks to keep the energy level up and the competition going. Picture having four or five fish on at the same time! Jigging in the winter is probably the most productive method of putting fish in the box. There is no question that once you have located the fish, you should be able to fill your limit in a short period of time. Because of this, many never learn the other means of bringing home Kokanee such as trolling.

Jigging can be as intense as it can be frustrating. Once you locate the fish, it takes a good eye and a feel for the strike. Mike Mansker, a fellow Kokanee fanatic; describes the process of a gold fish sucking in a food pellet and then spitting it out several times before actually swallowing the pellet. Picture your line running down fifty or more feet with a fluttering lead jig on the end. You raise the rod and let it fall, trying to keep enough tension on the line so you can sense the subtle bite of a fish sampling the bait and then spitting it out. You have a very brief opportunity to set the hook and initially you will miss it more than you will get it. By learning to watch the rod tip and developing a feel for the rod you will increase your catch rate significantly. I find that after a few short hours of jigging, I simply have to take a break. I get so involved in sensing the bite; I am emotionally drained at the end of the day. So much for a relaxing day of fishing! That is one reason that I will troll the second half of the day if I don't limit out early, to kind of cool down before heading home.

I will almost always use gel or scent on my jigs. By doing so, I create a cloud of scent around my jig. As the currents of water move by, the scent is carried along attracting more fish to my presentation. There are several good brands of scent on the market and I have tried many of them. My go-to gel at this point is ProCure. I love the stuff; I would even use it for aftershave if my wife would let me. The stuff is terribly sticky when you get it on your hands but once applied to a jig will last all day. My go-to scent for this time of year is Crayfish and has been responsible for many fish making the visit to my fish box. That being said, the scent that I will be using will be the one that is catching fish!

The Jeremy Jahn family with a nice catch of late summer Kokanee. Note: some of the fish are starting to turn pink indicating the end of the summer
Photo courtesy of Jeremy Jahn

LIGHTBULB MOMENT ☼ during the late fall and winter I use ocean scents such as Crayfish, Shrimp and Krill. During the summer typical lake type scents seem to work best.

One of the nice features of jigging is that you can have more people fishing at once than you would normally have while trolling. This can really add to the family aspect. Young kids catching fish right alongside the adults can lead to some pretty steep competition and generally just a lot of fun all around with multiple fish on at any one time. Sometimes it even gets so busy it is hard to keep track of how many fish you have in the boat!

Fishing with Bait:

One of the misnomers of Kokanee fishing is that the fish don't feed during the winter. Studies have shown that this is simply not true. If there is forage available, the fish will take advantage of it. So, depending on the weather, ice cover, and water temperature the amount of activity can vary widely. Bait is simply a very effective means of catching fish once you locate them and can be less intensive than just jigging for them in a traditional manner.

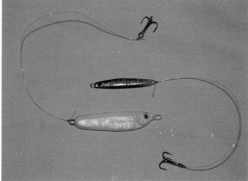

These jigs are set up for bait fishing. Note: a 30" heavy leader above the jig will help to keep the hooks from tangling in your line when dropping to depth.

The bait fishing setup I prefer is to remove the hook from a jig that is proportionate in size to the depth I am fishing, attaching a short fifteen to twenty pound leader and a treble to that. LIGHTBULB MOMENT ☼ on the upper end, I like to run a leader of the same weight, twenty four to thirty inches long to a swivel where my main line attaches. The stiffer leader below the jig body keeps the bait out in the open where fish can target it. The leader above keeps the limp braided main line from getting fouled up in the hook or jig because it is stiff enough to remain fairly straight.

Lower your jig to the depth of the school you are targeting or just above. The jig body will be visible on a good quality fish finder so you can track your jig in relation to the school you are targeting. Once you have reached the appropriate depth, sit motionless watching the rod tip and feeling for any indication of a strike. Some like to jig the offering up and down, but in reality is not bait fishing it is just jigging. Once the fish hone in on your bait, you will notice the bite will really turn on the longer you sit in a location. The cloud of scent put off by your bait will contribute to this and as such it is very important you spend some time preparing your baits the day or evening before heading out to the lake.

Corn is still my go-to bait for this type of fishing although; there are a number of other baits which will work fine for this. One of which are the dough baits, Power Bait being at the top of the list in popularity or possibly Yum. If you should use dough bait, be sure to get a few different colors and try to always get the ones which have sparkle as an ingredient. The sparkle may not work for the fish but it sure looks cool to me!

When preparing your corn, pay attention to the section on scents at the end of chapter 2. Once again, no matter what scent you use with your bait, mix a UV enhancer with that. I have also had very good luck using dyes with my corn. Some days, blue is the hot color and some days green is hot while sometimes natural or red is the go-to color. My point in this is, it does pay to take a variety of colors and scents because you never know what they will be biting on. An inexpensive scent I use quite often is garlic. I just shake a generous amount in a baggie with some corn the night before heading out and mix it up real well then stick it in the refrigerator. My wife is a lot more forgiving of this type of bait as opposed to meal worms and night crawlers in the vegetable drawer. Fortunately, I now have my own refrigerator out in my shop which I store my bait in. She is happy and I now have a spot for my beer...

Assorted Shasta Tackle Sling Blade dodgers

Bait which is often overlooked on a regular basis is cocktail shrimp. Not only do cocktail shrimp provide a very good scent of their own, but they can be treated much like corn by adding additional scent and dye. Make sure you buy fresh or frozen and just make up enough that you can use them before they spoil. If you think that rancid shrimp smells bad, just think how a fish which has a sense of smell 150 times greater than a bloodhound feels about your offering. Be sure and wash your hands every time you handle your terminal tackle! If you don't, you may be running off more fish than you are catching!

For all bait, I make it a policy to keep a cooler with ice whether fishing in cool weather or warm weather. Bait will retain better scent quality if it is kept cool or cold. I am sure in some areas the cooler would serve in the reverse keeping the bait from freezing before use, but that is not the case in my neck of the woods.

In this chapter, we have covered late fall and winter fishing in general. I much prefer to target other species during the late fall simply because the spawning fish are not in their prime for table fare and it really ticks me off to see so-called sportsmen out there killing fish that are not suitable table fare! However, once the spawn is over, and I am getting cabin fever from sitting by the fire or typing over a hot keyboard, there is nothing like a day out on the lake trolling or jigging for one of the Northwest's premier game fish. It doesn't matter whether it is raining, snowing or the sun is shining, I still get excited on the way up to the lake. If you dress appropriately, and use a little caution, you can have as much if not more fun than during the nicer weather. Speaking of weather, there are many days out on the lake in the dead of winter when it is just gorgeous. One of the bigger bonuses is that you will not be competing with water skiers and jet skis. Chances are you will have the entire lake all to yourself! I hope you will enjoy this fishery as much as I have over the years and that you will share it with friends and family as well!

*Nilo Phillips; **the smile says it all!***
photo courtesy of his uncle Jeremy Jahn

7 ...Making your own tackle

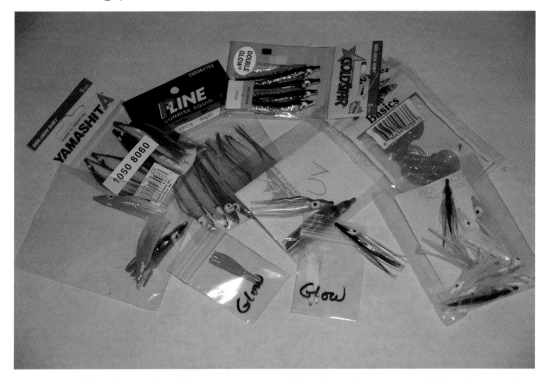

Assorted hoochie bodies. There are many suppliers/manufacturers available. Get a good selection by building your stash one bag at a time and pretty soon you will have more than you can use...

On a trip I took early on when starting this book I tied up approximately 150 different spinners and hoochies. My wife remarked that it would take me years to fish all of those lures. Most of those lures were gone during the course of the summer, used until the leaders were undependable or one of the hooks was lost. I also gave gear away to guys I met on the ramp or out on the lake. I always try to give a few instructions on their proper use when I do give them away but people seem to have a hard time taking or following directions. Most of those lures produced fish and in the process helped to improve my future lures. Many of the lures I tied up this spring were hoochies.

It is always fun to take a lure and improve on it by adding something which changes it from a producing lure into a great producing lure after all, thinking outside the box is the key to being successful if you want to make your own lures!

Tying up multiple hook sets is the beginning of the lure building process, whether you are making up spinners or hoochies. Most people who tie spinners and hoochies professionally use a fly-tying vise. You can purchase a vise from between twenty and a hundred a fifty bucks depending on your budget. I personally do not use a vise, preferring to just use my fingers. It takes some practice, but after a while you can pretty much tie up a set in the dark. The reason I

Mack's Lures Pip's Leader Caddy. Stick the hook in the cork, replace the lid and reel in the loose end. When you need a leader, choose one and pull it out. NO Tangles. This is Way Cool!

do that is because you never know when you will need to whip something up to match the hatch so to speak. I do try to keep several sets tied up in a leader caddy. This ingenious device will keep your spare leaders from getting tangled in a nice compact container and ready for use.

Snelling Hooks:

I prefer to use the snell knot when putting together my leaders. The reason for this is it not

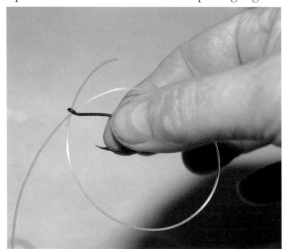

Detail 1: Pass your line down through the eye and back through forming a loop. Then grasp the eye and pinch the line with your right hand. Slide two fingers of your left hand through the loop and pull the loop back making loops around the shank of the hook.

only is it a solid dependable knot but it keeps the hooks in line and since double hook rigs are usually preferred for Kokanee this is an ideal setup. I personally tie the bottom hook first, snelling it with seven to ten wraps of good quality monofilament around the hook shank (see Detail 1 and Detail 2 below). I then take the free end of the leader and slide it up through the bottom of the eye of the upper hook. I then take the free end and run it around the eye and back through forming a loop large enough to loop around the hook which has already been tied. Holding the second hook between the thumb and forefinger of my left hand I adjust the bottom hook so there is just the right amount of space between the two hooks. Then taking the right hand and inserting the first two fingers in the loop which was formed I make between six and ten turns on the upper hook. Once that has been accomplished I grip the shank and the loops which have been made with the thumb and forefinger of my right hand and gently pull the free end until the knot is snug. I then finish off by holding the lower hook in my right hand and giving the free end a tug (See Detail 3).

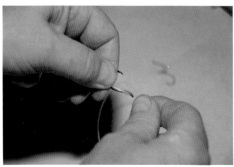

Detail 2: Holding the hook and whipped end of the line snuggly in your left hand give the other end a good tug with your right hand to firmly tighten the knot.

The leaders can then be turned onto the leader caddy. Quality hooks are very important! Spend your money on thin wire hooks either drop shot or octopus in the size of choice. My preferred hook is the Gamakatsu red drop shot in #4. I also use their red octopus hooks in #4. Depending on the lake and the time of year I will also vary the hook size. There are several other brands of hooks on the market today which are comparable to the Gamakatsu but I am getting old and kind of set in my ways so I will probably stick to my proven favorite until they either become unavailable or their quality goes down.

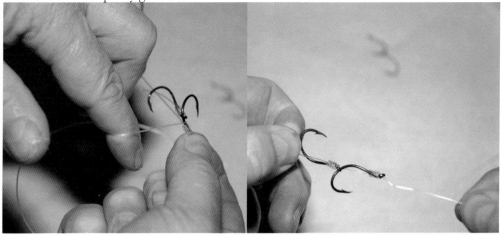

Detail 3: Take the upper free end of your leader and slide it through the upper hook eye from the bottom, around and back through forming a loop. Then use two fingers of your left hand to spin six or more loops around the upper hook shank as shown then pull until tight.

When tying up hoochies or spinners, I will first thread the free end through the eye of a needle which makes assembling your lure of choice much faster and in the case of hoochies much less frustrating. Once you have the needle threaded with your line, it is just a simple matter of threading on your beads or spacers of choice, and the needle readily penetrates the head of the hoochie, a task that is otherwise difficult at best. I also keep a couple of needles in my tackle box for those times out on the water when I need to make up something.

Hoochies:

When tying hoochies, I will use a bead just above the hook and then thread a piece of tubing and another bead. I have found the little tubes bobber stops come tied on work exceptionally well for this purpose. You want a bead on top of the hooks to keep the tube from sliding down over the upper hook. The bead on top of the tube keeps the sharp end of the tube from cutting a hole in the top of your hoochie when a fish wraps up in your line. I also use assorted beads instead of the tube to add color to clear hoochies. Glow beads work exceptionally well for this

A couple of hand-tied hoochies

purpose adding a whole new dimension to the hoochie craze. Another cool trick is to slide on a small bead over the hoochie head and then a clevis and blade of choice.

When buying bulk hoochies, be sure to buy double glow and UV. I have also had good results with sparkles which are embedded in the hoochie body. As you can see from the photo at the beginning of this chapter, there are many sources of hoochies or mini squids so whenever you spot one that looks like it may work, just add it to your collection and you will have years of entertainment ahead of you both at home and out on the water. Every little bit helps when you are trying to attract fish. The more tools you have in your box, the more likely you will have a successful day on the water!

One of the products I swear by is the Smile Blade sold by Mack's Lure. Putting a single bead in front of a hoochie and adding a smile blade can make the jump from good to great. Try bending the blades unevenly so the spin is erratic and watch out! Run this with a longer leader (18 inches or more) so the dodger doesn't impair the action.

LIGHTBULB MOMENT ☼ I have had good luck with cutting one of the wings off of a

Spin N Glow and running that in front of a hoochie of contrasting color with a small bead in between. The out of balance spin causes the hoochie to wobble and have an action of its own not to mention the flash of the Mylar wing as it spins around. You can run this combination as you would a spoon or other lure with a longer leader of eighteen inches or more. Spin-N-Glows are also now available with UV.

When tying up hoochies and spinners, I usually make up five or six of each and store them on a short section of foam pipe insulation tubing until I need them out on the water. I also carry boxes of beads, blades and clevises with me just in case I need to make something up to match the bite. If someone in another boat is having luck with something out on the lake, chances are I can readily match what it is they are using and sometimes improve on it.

Spinners:

When purchasing beads, check out the craft stores, you can pick up some real cool beads for next to nothing compared to the beads you buy at a sporting goods store. Some things to look for are faceted glass beads in assorted colors. Glass beads seem to refract the light better than their plastic counterparts. I am always on the lookout for glow beads. I cannot stress this enough, glow will increase your chances of bringing fish to the boat! You can also pick up beads at many of the larger sporting outfitters like Cabela's and Sportsman's Warehouse.

Blades are another thing it pays to shop around for! Cheap blades are not worth the effort to tie up. I bought some blades from a major supplier a few years ago and stored them in one of my boxes for the next opportunity to incorporate them into a lure. The box got exposed to moisture while fishing one day and the blades rusted. I didn't pay a whole lot for them but it would have really ticked me off had I spent a lot of time tying them up only to find they were worthless and needed to be thrown away. I try and find blades with good quality plating. That is not always possible but that is my ultimate goal. If some blades look questionable, I will lightly coat them with some clear lacquer to stave off corrosion.

I will also purchase blades which are painted with glow and fluorescent coating. I have had very good luck using blades of this nature. Try to buy a selection of sizes and styles, because who knows when you will stumble across something that is hotter than a Cajun spice rack! For example laying out a bunch of blades bottom side up and painting them black with aerosol paint will work wonders over normal unpainted blades when nothing else seems to work

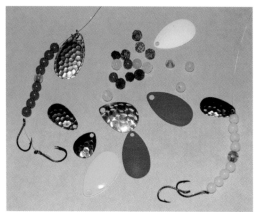

An assortment of beads, blades and (2) hand tied spinners

I find many hours of enjoyment on those long winter evenings just sitting at the dining room table and tying up tackle. I prefer not to sit in front of the TV for extended periods so this helps to pass away the time until I can get out and wet a line. Kids also seem to like putting together spinners, combining various colored beads and assorted blades to come up with that magical combination. It will also add to the excitement when they actually catch fish on a lure they put together with their own hands! Keep your eyes open for parts and pieces to put together your own little tackle kit. Start out by buying a few containers to separate beads and blades in an organized fashion and just keep adding to it over the long run. You will be surprised at how much tackle you can accumulate at a very reasonable cost.

Organization:

For storing your spinners and lures, make a trip to your local building supply. I buy the smaller diameter pipe insulation which just happens to come in six foot lengths and costs about a buck. I bought the storage boxes in the same spot, only in another section. I cut the pipe insulation to fit the boxes. I wrap the trailing end of the leader first, overlapping it with the leader that follows keeping a little tension then set the hooks of the lure into the foam. You can write on the box a general description of what type of lure is contained within to speed

changing out when you are in a hot bite. The cool thing is you won't be spending your time untangling your leaders every time you need something.

Another cool idea is to buy a CD wallet and keep your gang trolls separated by the individual CD holders. Just coil up your gang troll and slide it into one of the vinyl holders. No more tangled mess when you are trying to get your lines out at or just before daylight!

There is no limit to how crafty you can get when dealing with tackle. You can devise all manner of fish catching equipment if you are so inclined. You can also organize your tackle so it is easy to find what you are looking for in short order. Once you break the dependence barrier and start experimenting, you will be amazed at what not only catches fish but catches fish well! Many of those in the tackle business today started out by experimenting out of necessity. I am not suggesting you get into the tackle business, but I am suggesting you can experiment and have fun!

8 ...Care & Prep of the Catch

Fishing is a multifaceted sport in that it covers two of my favorite topics; catching and eating. I

Photo courtesy of Jeremy Jahn

get to go out and fish all day, enjoying the lake, the weather, companionship and excitement of the catch. The beauty is that it doesn't stop there! When I get home, I can have some of the best food money can't buy; Kokanee! Kokanee is mild by salmon standards and is a favorite of all who target them. Most that target them prefer them to any other fish commonly caught out of the lake such as trout and char. The key to this whole process is the care you give your catch from the moment you take it off the hook.

Proper care will keep the family coming back for more when they are presented at the dinner table. If you care for your catch poorly, you may be the only one interested in eating your catch and then only because you caught it. There are many who fish but never keep their catch, preferring to give it to others once the day is done. The first step in caring for your catch is to bleed it. Breaking a gill plate will accomplish that just fine. I prefer to poke a knife tip between the pectoral fins and slice forward. There is an immediate rush of blood and the fish is bled dry. I keep a sharp fillet knife in the back of the boat just for this purpose, washing it after every use. We usually leave the fish in the motor well for a few minutes before transferring them to a cooler full of ice. When fishing in a tournament, we add water to the ice and create slurry. In the case of tournament fishing bleeding your catch is avoided to retain weight.

As a kid growing up in central Oregon, we often kept our fish on a stringer suspended in the lake. At that time, we didn't give it much thought, but many times the water we were fishing in during the summer months was just like bath water. Needless to say, the warmer the weather the worse the fish tasted. We had all nature of ideas cooked up to keep the fish cool, but the only real effective method is to bleed them and get them packed in ice as quickly as possible.

Filleting:

At the end of the day, I prefer to fillet any fish which is over twelve inches. My preferred method is to use a piece of CDX plywood that I picked up at a local building supply. The plywood is two feet long and a foot and a half wide which easily fits in my truck or in my boat. Plywood helps to hold the fish stationary while you are cleaning them as opposed to the stainless steel found at most cleaning stations. I just lay my fish down on the plywood and make a cut down the back just behind the head to the backbone and then down to just behind the pectoral fin before turning the knife and running it back towards the tail following the spine. Once that fillet is done, I flip the fish over and do the other side. After you have become proficient at this method, the entrails will remain with the head to be deposited in the trash. I almost always try and do my cleaning in the field rather than have fish guts in the trash at home. This helps me to stay in good graces with my wife. Due to the small size of the bones in Kokanee, getting all of the bones out is usually futile, at least for me. I am not patient enough to work them out as I would a Chinook salmon or a Steelhead. If you choose to lift them out, lay the fillet cavity side up and slide the knife beneath the ribs resting your hand on the top of the ribs, slide the knife down towards the belly lifting all of the ribs out in one smooth operation. It is quite simple to remove the balance of the ribs once the fish are cooked. Smaller fish or at least those fewer than twelve inches are just gutted and scaled.

Once I am done with all of the fillets, I will rinse them off in the sink provided at the lake or in a bucket which I keep in my boat just for that purpose. I then put them in zip lock baggies and back in the ice chest they go for the ride home. Once home, I will keep the fillets on ice until I decide what it is I am going to do with them. Whether I am going to smoke them or fry them, or just freeze them for future meals, I prefer to skin my fillets. Some do this with a fillet knife but I use a Thompson fish skinner pictured to the right. It is a remarkably simple tool which will readily peel away the skin from multiple fish in short order. You just grip the skin near the tail, clamp down with the plier like handle with the left hand and turn the crank with your right hand. Instant skinned fish ready for the next step which would be freezing, smoking or eating.

Townsend Fish Skinner. This is a really cool little tool which is common to the East Coast. I picked mine up on EBay for about $12.00 used.

Beer Batter:

There is almost nothing better than Kokanee fried up in a good beer batter! The following is a simple recipe I use when craving some fried Kokanee!

- 1 cup all purpose flour
- 1 teaspoon salt
- 1 teaspoon baking powder
- 1 teaspoon garlic
- 2 teaspoons onion powder
- ½ teaspoon dried dill
- 1 can of beer (I prefer a can of good dark beer, not the cheap stuff but any old beer will work!)
- ½ cup of milk
- 2 whole eggs
- enough vegetable oil to submerge your fillets

Directions:

In a large bowl combine all of the ingredients but the oil. Mix well!

Place fillets in batter coating thoroughly. Let the fillets stand for between fifteen and twenty minutes.

Place oil in a large frying pan or deep fryer and bring to 375 degrees. Place fillets in oil and fry until golden brown. Do not add all of the fish at the same time or you will drop the temperature of the oil. Instead add the fish in batches. You can cook up some French fried potatoes in the same hot oil if you prefer. Serve up with some of your favorite vegetables and some tartar sauce and malt vinegar.

Smoking:

In preparation for smoking, the fish need to be brined. Brines come in two types: dry pack and wet. Dry pack brines are just that, no liquid added and usually have a combination of sugar and salt and herbs. Rock salt also works well for those who don't like their fish too salty.

Due to the large crystals, rock salt will not contact the fish as thoroughly as pickling salt. The ticket here is to just lay down a layer of rock salt followed by a layer of fish and another layer of rock salt. With this method, I usually cut the brine time down to an hour or so. My wife is rather salt intolerant so if I want company at the dinner table I have to comply. Another simple dry brine is two parts brown cane sugar and one part pickling salt. The system is the same, just pack your fish with the mixture and let stand for a couple of hours.

Kokanee Brine (my favorite!)

- 2 quarts water
- 2 cups brown sugar
- ¼ Cup pickling salt
- 2 table spoons granulated garlic
- 3 table spoons Tabasco sauce

Directions:

Heat water in a large container then blend ingredients. Let cool. Place fish (filleted or whole) in non-reactive container flesh to flesh starting with the bottom skin down. Add brine as the layers are completed so you get a good coat on every layer. Brine overnight in refrigerator. Place in smoker without drying or washing. Smoke till done (depends on temperature) at low setting, preferably under 150 degrees. My smoker is gas powered so it has a higher temp than some of the electric models.

Dry Pack Kokanee Brine:

Mix 1 part pickling salt and two parts dark brown sugar in a large mixing bowl. Start by putting a layer of the mixture in the bottom of the non-reactive container. Pack fish flesh to flesh taking care to completely cover the fish in the brine. Leave in mixture at least three hours prior to smoking. The timing will vary per your personal taste. A little experimentation will be required to achieve the perfect flavor you are seeking! I guess it means you are going to have to spend some more time fishing in order to perfect this recipe... Oh dang!

Once the fish is done smoking, I let it cool on wire racks prior to freezing or canning. I don't like my fish too dry so I may pull it from the smoker sooner than some. You will just have to play this by trial and error.

My preferred method of storing my smoked fish is to vacuum pack it and put it in the freezer for use down the road. When I am headed out hunting or fishing I will throw a package in my cooler to munch on during the course of the trip. It is much better for you than the processed foods you can buy in the store, not to mention it tastes a whole lot better!

Canning:

I also like to can some of my catch for future use. I personally prefer the fish is smoked prior to canning although that is not necessary. Once the fish has been removed from the smoker, pack it in hot sterile wide mouth pint jars, bones and all. I use a canning funnel to keep the fish from touching the rims of the jars and reducing the mess.

Pack the jars tightly to within an inch of the top of the jars then fill the jars with either hot distilled water or olive oil no closer than an inch from the top. Use a kitchen knife or other implement to work out any air bubbles that may be trapped in the jars.

Wipe down the rims of the jars with a clean towel to remove any oil or other debris which may be there. Keep a small pan of water boiling on the stove with the lids ready to cap the jars. Using a magnetic lid tool take the hot jar lids out and put them in the rings then tighten them down snugly on the jars.

Place the jars in a preheated pressure cooker as per the directions which came with your cooker. Bring the pressure to 15 lbs and keep it there for an hour and ten minutes. Let the cooker cool down until there is no pressure left before opening.

Place the jars on the counter until cool, before moving. Make sure all of the jars have sealed prior to storing them away!

Once you get around to using the canned fish, you will find it is every bit as good as canned tuna or salmon you would buy in the store. Any recipe which calls for tuna will be equally as good with canned Kokanee if not better!

Kokanee Casserole:

- 8 ounces of noodles
- 1 pint jar of smoked canned Kokanee
- 1 1/2 cups of sour cream
- 1 can of sliced mushrooms (drained)
- 2 cups of frozen peas
- 1 cup of grated cheddar cheese
- 1/4-1/2 cup of chopped jalapeno peppers (optional)
- 3/4 cup of milk
- 1 1/2 teaspoons salt
- 1/2 teaspoon Pepper
- 1/4 cup dry Italian bread crumbs
- 1/4 cup of grated Parmesan cheese
- 2 tablespoons butter or margarine

Directions:
Heat oven to 350 degrees. Cook noodles as directed on package. Combine cooked noodles, thawed peas, and remaining ingredients with the exception of bread crumbs, Parmesan cheese, and butter in a 3 quart casserole.

Mix bread crumbs, melted butter and Parmesan cheese then sprinkle over casserole. Bake uncovered 35-40 minutes or until done.

Smoked Kokanee in Cream Sauce over Fettuccine:

- 1 cup smoked Kokanee
- 1/2 cup butter
- 3/4 cup whipping cream
- 3/4 cup milk

- 1 cup grated Parmesan cheese
- 1 cup chopped fresh spinach
- 1 package of fettuccine noodles cooked and drained.

Directions:

De-bone smoked Kokanee fillets or use canned Kokanee then work into small flakes. Melt butter, add cream and milk stirring constantly. Thicken with corn starch. Blend balance of the ingredients. Toss with noodles and serve.

Creamy Kokanee Penne:

- 1 (16 ounce) package Penne pasta
- 2 tablespoons olive oil
- 1 teaspoon minced garlic
- 1 tomato, diced
- salt and pepper to taste
- 1 (8 ounce) package cream cheese
- ½ Pound smoked Kokanee de-boned and flaked.
- 2 tablespoons fresh finely chopped dill
- 1/4 cup chopped fresh basil
- 1/4 cup chopped fresh oregano
- 2 tablespoons chopped fresh parsley
- 1 bunch of fresh spinach washed and chopped.

Directions:

Bring a large pot of salted water to a boil. Add pasta and cook for 8 to 10 minutes or until done; drain.

In a large saucepan over medium heat, heat olive oil. Stir in garlic, basil, oregano, parsley, tomato, salt and pepper, and cook 5 minutes. Stir in cream cheese until melted. Add Kokanee and spinach. Heat through, serve over cooked pasta and garnish with fresh Italian parsley and Parmesan cheese.

~Good Investments~

Probably the best investments which you can make for your fishing adventures are a good means of storing your catch. The two items that follow are for the serious sportsman. Whether you use them yourself or your wife uses them, they will pay for themselves by preserving your catch for many tasty meals in the future.

A good vacuum packer will definitely pay for itself, not only for storing your wild game but for your domestic food as well. Good vacuum packers usually start at around fifty dollars and go up from there. Most people will never realize the investment for some of the more expensive models. I picked mine up on sale, and it has seen some serious use since its purchase. I was originally given one by my dad that he found at a yard sale. I used that one until the vacuum pump wouldn't work anymore. I buy large rolls of bag material and just cut the size I need for the product I am planning on freezing.

I borrowed an old pressure canner from a fishing buddy when I first started canning my catch. It didn't have a pressure gauge, only a metal weight to regulate the pressure. I was never sure whether or not I had the right pressure so I was always a little leery of the product. I finally broke down and bought a nice unit with a gauge so I was sure I was getting enough pressure for my fish. I picked it up on sale and only paid sixty bucks for it. I am sure it is possible to find a unit at a yard sale which would do the same thing at half the cost.

Preserving you catch does not have to be one of those chores you dread! A few simple tools purchased over time will enable you to enjoy your catch into the future. Hit the yard sales and look on EBay and Craigslist for the items you need. Keep an eye on the sales at your local department stores and you will be surprised at the deals you will come up with!

Remember, meal preparation starts when you land that fish. From that point on it can be either a good meal or a barely edible meal. Care and cleaning of your catch will add enjoyment never before experienced.

When I was a kid growing up in rural Oregon, we raised much of our own food and in the process we named our farm animals. The dinner discussion went something like, "Mom, are we eating Spotty or Frisky tonight?" When you are dining on your fish from a trip over to Wallowa Lake, Wickiup or any other lake of choice in California, Oregon, Washington, Idaho or any state where you reside or fish; the conversation will soon turn to the time you had there and plans for the future! The conversation may also include the friends you made along the way since, at least in my experience; kokaholics are a friendly group always willing to share. Hopefully I will see you out there on the lake somewhere while working on my next meal!

Tight Lines and Good Fishing!

Wallowa Lake with a spring storm blowing in

9 ...Resources; Contact info for tackle suppliers

The following links and resources will give you the reader a variety of resources to find tackle and components to pursue this sport. By all means buy local if at all possible! With the influx of larger chain stores, many of the mom and pop stores are driven out of business. With their loss, we lose much more than just a source of tackle!

The Author's website

Updates and more fishing resources: http://kentcannon.com/

Manufacturers:

1. Abu Garcia: http://www.abugarcia.com/
   Makers of solid quality reels suitable for Kokanee fishing.

2. Acme Tackle Company: http://www.acmetackle.com
   Makers of the Little Cleo spoon

3. Crystal Basin Tackle and Guide Service: http://www.crystalbasintackle.com/
   Makers and suppliers of quality handmade Kokanee fishing gear and just fine people to deal with!

4. Fishing With Father Murphy: http://www.fishingwithfathermurphy.com/
   Check out the unique Kokanee bugs and awesome spinners!

5. Hot Spot Lures: http://www.hotspotlures.com/
   Makers of the famous and extremely effective Apex spoons!

6. Lamiglas: http://www.lamiglas.com/
   Makers of quality fishing rods!

7. Luhr-Jensen http://www.luhrjensen.com/
   Makers of the Krocodile and Needlefish spoons

8. Mack's Lure: http://www.mackslure.com/
   Makers of the Wedding Ring, Cha Cha and the Double D dodger and assorted lure making materials.

9. Offshore Tackle Co.: http://www.offshoretackle.com/
   Makers of great side planers and downrigger releases.

10. Okuma: http://www.okumafishingteam.com/
    Makers of good quality reasonably priced Kokanee rods and Reels

11. Sep's Pro fishing: http://www.sepsprofishing.com/
    Makers of quality Kokanee tackle including dodgers, spoons, flashers and downrigger releases.

12. Shasta Tackle Company: http://shastatackle.com/Originators of the Cripple Lure and Hum Dinger, Shuttle Hawk and the Sling Blade Dodger.

13. Tica: http://www.ticaamerica.com/
    Makers of rods and reels suitable for Kokanee

14. Pautzke Bait Company: http://www.pautzke.com/
    Makers of Fire Corn, Balls O Fire, and Kokanee Fuel

15. ProCure Bait Scents: http://www.pro-cure.com/
    Makers of top quality scents, oils, and UV enhanced dyes

16. Pro-Troll Fishing Products: http://www.protroll.com/
    Makers of the Kokanee Killer spoons and the Black Box electronic fish magnet

17. R&K Spinners: (541)220-1603
    Maker of hand dyed unique hoochies, Micro hoochies hand made spinners, custom lake trolls and custom tackle

18. Rocky Mountain Tackle (RMT): http://www.rockymountaintackle.com/
    Makers of Signature squid hoochies and other misc. tackle.

19. Scotty: http://www.scotty.com/
    Makers of quality downriggers and rod holders.

20. Vance's Tackle Company: http://www.vancestackle.com/
    Makers of top quality dodgers, flashers, spoons, ball trolls and spiral wrapped rods and much more.

Organizations:

1. Kokanee Power: http://www.Kokaneepower.org/
   Non profit organization providing support to the state fisheries and promoting the sport of Kokanee fishing.

2. Kokanee Power of Oregon: http://www.Kokaneepower.org/oregon/
   Non profit organization promoting the sport of Kokanee fishing in Oregon.

At Kokanee Power events kids fish for free making everyone a winner!

Suppliers:

1. Cabela's: http://www.cabelas.com/
   large chain with good mail order and destination shopping great for purchasing components.

2. Bi-Mart: http://www.bimart.com/
   Located throughout the Northwest, this chain carries a good assortment of tackle and accessories including Lamiglas rods, Shasta Tackle, and Hot-Spot Lures.

3. Dick's Sporting Goods: http://www.dickssportinggoods.com/
   Located throughout Oregon, Dick's carries a good selection of Kokanee gear from many of the makers listed above.

4. Kokanee Mart: http://store.Kokaneemart.com/
   One of the original online Kokanee tackle dealers with a good selection.

5. KokaneeTackle.com: http://www.Kokaneetackle.com/default.aspx
   Good assortment of Kokanee tackle and good prices

6. Fisherman's Marine & Outdoor: http://www.fishermans-marine.com/
   a great resource for the Northwest. Experienced staff and great selections!

7. Wholesale Sports: http://us.wholesalesports.com/
   Large chain with good selections

8. Sportsman's Warehouse: http://www.sportsmanswarehouse.com/
   Large chain with good selections

Wallowa Lake